The Whole Truth and Nothing But the Truth

by Diane Averill
and
Edith Bajema

2 LEADER GUIDES AND 10 DISCUSSION HANDOUTS

© 1995 by CRC Publications, 2850 Kalamazoo Ave. SE,
Grand Rapids, MI 49560.

Church
Development
Resources™

A Ministry of CRC Publications

ISBN 1–56212–108–1

10 9 8 7 6 5 4 3 2 1

Contents

Introduction to Inspirit

Whether this is your first time leading a small group or you are a veteran leader, welcome to the exciting world of small-group, evangelistic Bible study. These materials were written as an entry level for men and women who may never have studied the Bible before. Whether you are leading a group in your workplace, in your home, or another setting, the following guidelines should assist you in your leadership role.

1. PRAY

Nothing will prepare you for leadership more than prayer. Pray for God's direction in making organizational decisions. Pray for the Holy Spirit's direction in whom to invite and for a positive response from those invited. Pray faithfully for group members, and pray for your eyes to be opened to the truths in God's Word and how those truths can best be communicated to your small group. Remember: "More things are wrought by prayer than this world ever dreamed of."

2. PREPARE

Prepare Yourself. The leadership material for each discussion is thorough and reinforces the discovery method of Bible study. We suggest highlighting key phrases or questions for easy reference as you prepare. Take your leader material with you to the small group and be relaxed and informal about using it while you are leading. The perforated discussion copies, located behind the leader material, are to be removed and given to group members each week. If you freely show you have extra help in preparing for the discussion, your group members may dare to ask their questions more readily. They'll see it's not that you're smart and they're ignorant, or that the discussion is just an unguided free-for-all, but it is planned for and focused. Be sure you focus on the discussion element rather than become a teacher with the "answer book."

Decide whether you will use the **condensed** or the **expanded** format in your group. Time will determine your decision. The condensed format can be done over lunch in a 30- to 40-minute time period. The expanded format can take up to 90 minutes. The leader material includes additional help for use in the expanded format, and is marked with the symbol at right in the Leader Guide copy.

Prepare Your Group. State the ground rules before you begin the group and periodically to clarify or as new members join. This will help group members know how the discussion will proceed and know what will be expected of them. Some basic ground rules are:

We're here to see what the Bible has to say, not argue right or wrong.

No previous experience at studying the Bible is needed.

This discussion will not require homework or outside activities.

Respect the confidentiality of the group. "What we say here must stay here." We respect and affirm each group member.

3. PERSEVERE

It takes time to build relationships with non-Christians. The Holy Spirit will already have been at work in some people and they will respond eagerly. Others will be wary. Still others may be in such pain, they'll come because they are desperate. Accept the people God gives you—unconditionally. Often God's timetable is not the same as ours, but be confident that God will use your efforts. Modeling Christ's love may be the most important thing you do. Relax and watch the Spirit work!

The Whole Truth and Nothing But the Truth

1: The Truth About God

Introductory Notes

This *Inspirit* study is different from others in this series because it leans more toward the philosophical, theoretical, and theological. Although the topics are less needs-based, they are part of daily life. Newcomers to Bible study wrestle with these topics before they accept Christianity and the Bible as ultimate truth.

Renowned twentieth century philosopher Francis Schaeffer once said, "No man can live without a world view; therefore, there is no man who is not a philosopher." Our basic world view controls our actions. For example, our perception of God, the Bible, existence after death, and a final judgment all shape the ultimate choices we make.

We live in a pluralistic society. Our coworkers, neighbors, and sports companions hold divergent views on life's basic issues. No longer is belief in absolutes "politically correct." In fact, often the person who suffers discrimination is the one who dares to claim that absolute standards exist.

Furthermore, many people believe that contradictory religious views about God, the Bible, and the afterlife can all be true at the same time. Our culture says, "Because no one can prove God's existence, everyone is entitled to his or her own opinion. In that sense, everyone is right."

This *Inspirit* study covers topics that will no doubt generate opposing viewpoints. Individuals in your group will likely disagree on the issues. For this reason, keep some basic perspectives in mind.

Donald Posterski, in *Reinventing Evangelism,* states that in order to effectively reach people, believers must first pray, then care, and then communicate. Pray that God will send to your discussion sessions people who are open to learning more about him. Then pray that the Holy Spirit will work mightily in their lives.

Second, respect group members whose views are different from your own. Even the strongest disagreement should never propel you into an orbit of superiority. Many citizens of the kingdom today did not immediately believe the truth. Remember that your reaction to others' statements can leave strong and lasting impressions. Sometimes people will "raise red flags" in order to test your reaction. If you react defensively and negatively, they may reject your message. If, on the other hand, you are accepting and kind, they may listen further.

When the apostle Paul spoke to the Athenians (Acts 17), some believed right away, some rejected his message, and some wanted to hear more at another time. Have patience. Only after you have prayed for and cared for people will you be able to communicate the gospel to them. An inner-city teacher who often witnessed to his colleagues observed that caring for his coworkers personally was a more powerful testimony than his philosophical arguments.

Finally, do not allow these sessions to degenerate into a simple sharing of equally valid opinions. You will need to remind the group occasionally that you are presenting biblical truth rather than your own ideas. Allow members freedom to disagree. They must understand, however, that they disagree not with you personally, but with the Word of God.

Do not be intimidated if a group member asks a question you cannot answer. You can ask for time to think about it before you discuss the matter. This will give you the chance to consult your pastor or a helpful book on the subject. Books such as John Stott's *Basic Christianity* or C. S. Lewis' *Mere Christianity* are excellent sources for those who want to look deeper into some of the topics you discuss. If you need further preparation for this study, consider Donald Posterski's *Reinventing Evangelism* or *Why Should Anyone Believe Anything at All?* by James W. Sire.

Before you lead this lesson and ask the opening questions, take a personal inventory. Ask yourself how you view God. Do you try to style God in your image rather than allowing him to mold you into his? When God felt distant, was there a reason? Did you need to confess a sin or right a wrong? Pray that God will give you a new sense of his majesty and activity in human history. Think about what it means for you to "live and move and have your being" in him.

Beginning the Session

Welcome your group members warmly. Be low-key and relaxed. A Bible study may pose a threat to some of them, so work on building relationships based on trust. Let the group know—both verbally and nonverbally—that you respect them. Do all you can to make them comfortable. Share a little about yourself and set some simple goals for the time you will spend together. Say something like, "Over the next six weeks we'll be looking at some very basic teachings in the Bible to see if we can get a better understanding of what it's all about." Smile and relax. Your comfort will enhance theirs.

Beginnings

As a youngster, how did you first visualize God? For example, was he a Santa Claus figure? A judge? A grandfather? How has your view of God changed as you've gotten older?

Use these beginning questions to learn what group members believe concerning God and how their beliefs differ from Scripture. Their answers will help you know which of God's attributes to highlight during your discussion. For example, if many in your group view God as a harsh, unforgiving judge, ask them why they feel that way. **What happened to make them see God that way?** Highlight the truth: God desires a relationship with us. Tell them that God wants us to know him and has made a way (through Jesus Christ) for that to happen. He is not some distant, unfeeling deity, but rather a personal and relational being.

Remember that individuals in your group may believe in God but virtually ignore him. **Why does God seem to have so little to do with your life? Do you see God as supreme? What power do you think he has? If God has more power than people, why do some people ignore him? What would you like God to be in your life?** Use these questions to discern the group's needs. You do not have to respond to all they say. As you cover the questions, you might emphasize God as Creator, the one who has given us "life and breath" and the one to whom we are responsible.

 In the expanded format, encourage group members to share experiences that changed their understanding of God. **Was an event, a person, or a book most influential?**

What's Happening Today

As you read this section aloud, you will find that some of the responses that you received from your group in "Beginnings" will be echoed in these descriptions. Allow time for comments, but if you believe that discussion has been adequate, move into the reading of the passages. You might explain that one passage was written in the Old Testament part of the Bible by a man named Isaiah, and that the other passage comes from the New Testament, written after Jesus came. Point out also that both writers picked up on the creative power of God. You may wonder how many starry Palestinian skies they viewed.

What the Bible Tells Us

If you sense group members are comfortable reading aloud, ask for a volunteer. Read body language to determine whether someone is willing. Be sure to scan ahead during the reading to anticipate difficult names or words in the passage that the reader may need help with.

How the Bible Relates

1. How did Isaiah react when he saw the night sky?

Begin by exploring Isaiah's reaction to the night sky. What a fascinating way to describe God's creative power and control over the universe, that he even calls the stars by name. **What does this suggest about God's authority**

over nature? To name something indicates authority over it. Isaiah says that God completely controls the vast universe. The next passage will further cover God's creative power, so you do not need to spend much time on this question. Also, do not get bogged down in the *how* of creation; just stress that the passage indicates God did it.

 In the extended format, you might want to read to your group Isaiah 40:28-31 and discuss how God is still interested in our needs. He who is all-powerful and never weary will help us when we reach out to him. He promises to give strength and power when we need it. Note, however, that the basis of his gift is our "hoping in him."

2. Can you recall a time when you were awed by the night sky as Isaiah was? What was your response?

Everyone in your group will probably be able to describe how they felt when they gazed on the heavens and countless stars. **Why does this experience bring a sense of awe? Why might a person feel insignificant at that place and time?**

3. What does the passage from Acts 17 presume about God in its opening statement? How do you respond to this?

Before they can respond, your group needs to acknowledge that God created all and is over all. You may get a variety of answers to the second part of this question. Some in your group may believe that God is simply a "higher power" who set the world in motion but is not interested in its daily operation. Again, do not be bogged down with the *how* of creation, but look closely at what the passage says. **How does the speaker describe God? What do you think the phrase "the world and everything in it" includes? Would it also include human life—and you and me? If this is true, what might be our responsibility to God?** These verses state that "he himself gives all men life and breath and everything else." **What kind of ongoing care and interest by God does that imply?** Let group members wrestle with the issue of God's relationship to his creation—and the creation's response to its Creator.

You might also look at the phrase "Lord of heaven and earth." **What does a "lord" do? How might God be Lord of heaven and earth? What meaning might that have for our everyday lives?**

4. According to these verses, how has God made himself available to people?

Again, focus on the picture of God that we find in these verses. **As God has involved himself in human history, what has been his desire and purpose? What does he want people to do?** Your group members should pick up on God's longing to establish a relationship with the humans he created—including those in your group.

The Bible reveals God as a Creator who is not distant and unfeeling but rather, as John Stott puts it in *Basic Christianity,* a God who, long before it even occurs to man to turn to him, while man is still lost in darkness and sunk in sin, rises from his throne, lays aside his glory, and stoops to seek until he finds him.

God made us, and he set humankind down the pathway of history in order that we might look for him.

 In the longer format, you may want to look at Romans 1:19-20 with your group:

For the truth about God is known to [men] instinctively; God has put this knowledge in their hearts. Since earliest times men have seen the earth and sky and all God made, and have known of his existence and great eternal power.

Look at the evidence of God's eternal power in the starry sky, for example. **In what ways do people respond when they see the greatness of creation? What options do they have?** People can ignore the evidence and choose to believe that an impersonal being wound up the universe and then tossed it away to run on its own. They may try to shape God after their own finite imaginations. Or they might recognize him for who he is—not a God who is "watching us from a distance," as a popular song claims, but a God who comes to us "up close and personal."

The phrase "in him we live and move and have our being" might be misunderstood in the New Age sense, which teaches that God is in everything and everything is in God. A New Ager might ask, "If God is already in us, why would we have to reach out to him?" Explain that later sessions will deal with the things that have broken the relationship between God and humans and the great length to which God has gone in order to restore that relationship. For now, say God's intent, from the very beginning, was to have an intimate relationship with the people he created. But since humans broke off that relationship, we must seek God.

 In the longer format, you may want to discuss what it means to seek God. **What can a person do to develop a relationship with God?** Some obvious answers are prayer (communicating with God) and reading the Bible, which gives us teachings, stories, and insight from God. You might also explore some passages from the Bible that talk about the qualities of God's nature, for example, Psalm 103:8, 139:7-10, 147:5; Isaiah 6:3; John 4:24; 1 Timothy 1:17; Hebrews 4:13; and James 1:17.

5. In your experience today, would you describe God as being close or far away?

This question, like the one in "Beginnings," should show you what experiences have shaped your group members' concepts of God. Be sensitive to their struggles, especially if some have felt that God has been distant during illness or loss. Gently probe their responses if it's appropriate. Even those who think God is close to them may be misguided. Ask, **why do you think God seems close (or far away) to you?**

Even C. S. Lewis, a renowned Christian author and theologian, wrote in *A Grief Observed* that he felt as though God had locked and bolted the door during his wife's illness and death. Later Lewis discovered that, because of his grief, he was the one who had bolted the door from the inside. Listen to the experiences of various group members. Those who feel close to God because of all they are *doing* will learn some surprising truths in the lessons ahead. If you find it fitting, you might share Lewis's experience and insights with those who feel far away from God.

The Bottom Line

The vast universe points to a powerful and loving Creator. We can keep that Creator at a distance or we can seek ways to learn more about him. The choice is made easier by the fact that God desires for us to reach out and find him. He is not far from us!

Read this aloud with your group as a way of summarizing this session. Encourage them to open up their hearts for a relationship with God. Be alert for those who may already be open and ready to seek that relationship. Contact them during the week by phone or card to let them know you're thinking of them and to encourage them in their search for God. Do what you can to build a trusting relationship so that they will find it easy to come to you with their questions.

Optional Prayer Time

Use this closing prayer if it seems appropriate at this point in the discussion. Make your prayer time more personal than this simple closing prayer; however, be sure to save enough time at the end to ask about situations or problems for which group members may want prayer. This is an important element of your brief meeting time.

Your group members might share some of their struggles. Be supportive and look for ways that you or other members can assist and encourage them. Again, make certain that appropriate boundaries are maintained. You are not there to solve everyone's problems, but you might provide some practical assistance such as occasional child care, meals, transportation, lawn mowing. These can powerfully model the love of God for group members.

Prayer

God, we stand in awe of your creation. Help this fact to make a difference in our lives. Amen.

A Final Word

The earth is the Lord's, and everything in it. *(David in Psalm 24:1)*

1: The Truth About God

Beginnings

As a youngster, how did you first visualize God? For example, was he a Santa Claus figure? A judge? A grandfather? How has your view of God changed as you've gotten older?

What's Happening Today

Some pollsters estimate that as many as 96 percent of North Americans claim to believe in God. People hold many different views of God, however. In fact, some of these views contradict each other.

To Marla, God was a loving grandfather type who would come to her aid when she called him. She didn't have much to do with God until she needed something or got into trouble, and then she would pray. Sometimes God seemed to answer and sometimes he did not. Marla would often become upset when everything did not go exactly as she had planned. As she grew older, she blamed God for what went wrong in her life.

Brad, on the other hand, patterned his idea of God after his own father, who was distant and selfish. Brad had a hard time praying to God, because he thought that the Creator of the universe, like his dad, probably had no interest in him. Brad always felt that he had to manage his own life, and he never thought to consult God in his daily decisions.

Carlos always felt guilty. He pictured God as a judge in a black robe. He believed that God either gave him the "thumbs up" or the "thumbs down" sign, depending on what he did. Usually it was "thumbs down," he figured. Carlos never considered himself good enough to please God, so could not believe that God would love him.

The Bible shows these impressions of God to be wrong. The following passages from the Bible paint a true portrait of God and show what he is really like.

What the Bible Tells Us

"To whom will you compare me?
Or who is my equal?" says the Holy One.
Lift your eyes and look to the heavens:
Who created all these?
He who brings out the starry host one by one,
    and calls them each by name.
Because of his great power and mighty strength,
    not one of them is missing. (Isaiah 40:25-26)

The God who made the world and everything in it is the Lord of heaven and earth and does not live in temples built by hands. And he is not served by human hands, as if he needed anything, because he himself gives all men life and breath and everything else. From one man he made every nation of men, that they should inhabit the whole earth; and he determined the times set for them and the exact places where they should live. God did this so that men would seek him and perhaps reach out for him and find him, though he is not far from each one of us. "For in him we live and move and have our being." (Acts 17:24-28)

How the Bible Relates

1. How did Isaiah react when he saw the night sky?

2. Can you recall a time when you were awed by the night sky as Isaiah was? What was your response?

3. What does the passage from Acts 17 presume about God in its opening statement? How do you respond to this?

4. According to these verses, how has God made himself available to people?

5. In your experience today, would you describe God as being close or far away?

The Bottom Line

The vast universe points to a powerful and loving Creator. We can keep that Creator at a distance or we can seek ways to learn more about him. The choice is made easier by the fact that God desires for us to reach out and find him. He is not far from us!

Prayer

God, we stand in awe of your creation. Help this fact to make a difference in our lives. Amen.

A Final Word

The earth is the Lord's, and everything in it. *(David in Psalm 24:1)*

1: The Truth About God

Beginnings

As a youngster, how did you first visualize God? For example, was he a Santa Claus figure? A judge? A grandfather? How has your view of God changed as you've gotten older?

What's Happening Today

Some pollsters estimate that as many as 96 percent of North Americans claim to believe in God. People hold many different views of God, however. In fact, some of these views contradict each other.

To Marla, God was a loving grandfather type who would come to her aid when she called him. She didn't have much to do with God until she needed something or got into trouble, and then she would pray. Sometimes God seemed to answer and sometimes he did not. Marla would often become upset when everything did not go exactly as she had planned. As she grew older, she blamed God for what went wrong in her life.

Brad, on the other hand, patterned his idea of God after his own father, who was distant and selfish. Brad had a hard time praying to God, because he thought that the Creator of the universe, like his dad, probably had no interest in him. Brad always felt that he had to manage his own life, and he never thought to consult God in his daily decisions.

Carlos always felt guilty. He pictured God as a judge in a black robe. He believed that God either gave him the "thumbs up" or the "thumbs down" sign, depending on what he did. Usually it was "thumbs down," he figured. Carlos never considered himself good enough to please God, so could not believe that God would love him.

The Bible shows these impressions of God to be wrong. The following passages from the Bible paint a true portrait of God and show what he is really like.

What the Bible Tells Us

"To whom will you compare me?
Or who is my equal?" says the Holy One.
Lift your eyes and look to the heavens:
Who created all these?
He who brings out the starry host one by one,
*   and calls them each by name.*
Because of his great power and mighty strength,
*   not one of them is missing.* (Isaiah 40:25-26)

The God who made the world and everything in it is the Lord of heaven and earth and does not live in temples built by hands. And he is not served by human hands, as if he needed anything, because he himself gives all men life and breath and everything else. From one man he made every nation of men, that they should inhabit the whole earth; and he determined the times set for them and the exact places where they should live. God did this so that men would seek him and perhaps reach out for him and find him, though he is not far from each one of us. "For in him we live and move and have our being." (Acts 17:24-28)

How the Bible Relates

1. How did Isaiah react when he saw the night sky?

2. Can you recall a time when you were awed by the night sky as Isaiah was? What was your response?

3. What does the passage from Acts 17 presume about God in its opening statement? How do you respond to this?

4. According to these verses, how has God made himself available to people?

5. In your experience today, would you describe God as being close or far away?

The Bottom Line

The vast universe points to a powerful and loving Creator. We can keep that Creator at a distance or we can seek ways to learn more about him. The choice is made easier by the fact that God desires for us to reach out and find him. He is not far from us!

Prayer

God, we stand in awe of your creation. Help this fact to make a difference in our lives. Amen.

A Final Word

The earth is the Lord's, and everything in it. *(David in Psalm 24:1)*

1: The Truth About God

Beginnings

As a youngster, how did you first visualize God? For example, was he a Santa Claus figure? A judge? A grandfather? How has your view of God changed as you've gotten older?

What's Happening Today

Some pollsters estimate that as many as 96 percent of North Americans claim to believe in God. People hold many different views of God, however. In fact, some of these views contradict each other.

To Marla, God was a loving grandfather type who would come to her aid when she called him. She didn't have much to do with God until she needed something or got into trouble, and then she would pray. Sometimes God seemed to answer and sometimes he did not. Marla would often become upset when everything did not go exactly as she had planned. As she grew older, she blamed God for what went wrong in her life.

Brad, on the other hand, patterned his idea of God after his own father, who was distant and selfish. Brad had a hard time praying to God, because he thought that the Creator of the universe, like his dad, probably had no interest in him. Brad always felt that he had to manage his own life, and he never thought to consult God in his daily decisions.

Carlos always felt guilty. He pictured God as a judge in a black robe. He believed that God either gave him the "thumbs up" or the "thumbs down" sign, depending on what he did. Usually it was "thumbs down," he figured. Carlos never considered himself good enough to please God, so could not believe that God would love him.

The Bible shows these impressions of God to be wrong. The following passages from the Bible paint a true portrait of God and show what he is really like.

What the Bible Tells Us

"To whom will you compare me?
Or who is my equal?" says the Holy One.
Lift your eyes and look to the heavens:
Who created all these?
He who brings out the starry host one by one,
    and calls them each by name.
Because of his great power and mighty strength,
    not one of them is missing. (Isaiah 40:25-26)

The God who made the world and everything in it is the Lord of heaven and earth and does not live in temples built by hands. And he is not served by human hands, as if he needed anything, because he himself gives all men life and breath and everything else. From one man he made every nation of men, that they should inhabit the whole earth; and he determined the times set for them and the exact places where they should live. God did this so that men would seek him and perhaps reach out for him and find him, though he is not far from each one of us. "For in him we live and move and have our being." (Acts 17:24-28)

How the Bible Relates

1. How did Isaiah react when he saw the night sky?

2. Can you recall a time when you were awed by the night sky as Isaiah was? What was your response?

3. What does the passage from Acts 17 presume about God in its opening statement? How do you respond to this?

4. According to these verses, how has God made himself available to people?

5. In your experience today, would you describe God as being close or far away?

The Bottom Line

The vast universe points to a powerful and loving Creator. We can keep that Creator at a distance or we can seek ways to learn more about him. The choice is made easier by the fact that God desires for us to reach out and find him. He is not far from us!

Prayer

God, we stand in awe of your creation. Help this fact to make a difference in our lives. Amen.

A Final Word

The earth is the Lord's, and everything in it. *(David in Psalm 24:1)*

1: The Truth About God

Beginnings

As a youngster, how did you first visualize God? For example, was he a Santa Claus figure? A judge? A grandfather? How has your view of God changed as you've gotten older?

What's Happening Today

Some pollsters estimate that as many as 96 percent of North Americans claim to believe in God. People hold many different views of God, however. In fact, some of these views contradict each other.

To Marla, God was a loving grandfather type who would come to her aid when she called him. She didn't have much to do with God until she needed something or got into trouble, and then she would pray. Sometimes God seemed to answer and sometimes he did not. Marla would often become upset when everything did not go exactly as she had planned. As she grew older, she blamed God for what went wrong in her life.

Brad, on the other hand, patterned his idea of God after his own father, who was distant and selfish. Brad had a hard time praying to God, because he thought that the Creator of the universe, like his dad, probably had no interest in him. Brad always felt that he had to manage his own life, and he never thought to consult God in his daily decisions.

Carlos always felt guilty. He pictured God as a judge in a black robe. He believed that God either gave him the "thumbs up" or the "thumbs down" sign, depending on what he did. Usually it was "thumbs down," he figured. Carlos never considered himself good enough to please God, so could not believe that God would love him.

The Bible shows these impressions of God to be wrong. The following passages from the Bible paint a true portrait of God and show what he is really like.

What the Bible Tells Us

"To whom will you compare me?
Or who is my equal?" says the Holy One.
Lift your eyes and look to the heavens:
Who created all these?
He who brings out the starry host one by one,
*   and calls them each by name.*
Because of his great power and mighty strength,
*   not one of them is missing.* (Isaiah 40:25-26)

The God who made the world and everything in it is the Lord of heaven and earth and does not live in temples built by hands. And he is not served by human hands, as if he needed anything, because he himself gives all men life and breath and everything else. From one man he made every nation of men, that they should inhabit the whole earth; and he determined the times set for them and the exact places where they should live. God did this so that men would seek him and perhaps reach out for him and find him, though he is not far from each one of us. "For in him we live and move and have our being." (Acts 17:24-28)

How the Bible Relates

1. How did Isaiah react when he saw the night sky?

2. Can you recall a time when you were awed by the night sky as Isaiah was? What was your response?

3. What does the passage from Acts 17 presume about God in its opening statement? How do you respond to this?

4. According to these verses, how has God made himself available to people?

5. In your experience today, would you describe God as being close or far away?

The Bottom Line

The vast universe points to a powerful and loving Creator. We can keep that Creator at a distance or we can seek ways to learn more about him. The choice is made easier by the fact that God desires for us to reach out and find him. He is not far from us!

Prayer

God, we stand in awe of your creation. Help this fact to make a difference in our lives. Amen.

A Final Word

The earth is the Lord's, and everything in it. *(David in Psalm 24:1)*

1: The Truth About God

Beginnings

As a youngster, how did you first visualize God? For example, was he a Santa Claus figure? A judge? A grandfather? How has your view of God changed as you've gotten older?

What's Happening Today

Some pollsters estimate that as many as 96 percent of North Americans claim to believe in God. People hold many different views of God, however. In fact, some of these views contradict each other.

To Marla, God was a loving grandfather type who would come to her aid when she called him. She didn't have much to do with God until she needed something or got into trouble, and then she would pray. Sometimes God seemed to answer and sometimes he did not. Marla would often become upset when everything did not go exactly as she had planned. As she grew older, she blamed God for what went wrong in her life.

Brad, on the other hand, patterned his idea of God after his own father, who was distant and selfish. Brad had a hard time praying to God, because he thought that the Creator of the universe, like his dad, probably had no interest in him. Brad always felt that he had to manage his own life, and he never thought to consult God in his daily decisions.

Carlos always felt guilty. He pictured God as a judge in a black robe. He believed that God either gave him the "thumbs up" or the "thumbs down" sign, depending on what he did. Usually it was "thumbs down," he figured. Carlos never considered himself good enough to please God, so could not believe that God would love him.

The Bible shows these impressions of God to be wrong. The following passages from the Bible paint a true portrait of God and show what he is really like.

What the Bible Tells Us

"To whom will you compare me?
Or who is my equal?" says the Holy One.
Lift your eyes and look to the heavens:
Who created all these?
He who brings out the starry host one by one,
*   and calls them each by name.*
Because of his great power and mighty strength,
*   not one of them is missing.* (Isaiah 40:25-26)

The God who made the world and everything in it is the Lord of heaven and earth and does not live in temples built by hands. And he is not served by human hands, as if he needed anything, because he himself gives all men life and breath and everything else. From one man he made every nation of men, that they should inhabit the whole earth; and he determined the times set for them and the exact places where they should live. God did this so that men would seek him and perhaps reach out for him and find him, though he is not far from each one of us. "For in him we live and move and have our being." (Acts 17:24-28)

How the Bible Relates

1. How did Isaiah react when he saw the night sky?

2. Can you recall a time when you were awed by the night sky as Isaiah was? What was your response?

3. What does the passage from Acts 17 presume about God in its opening statement? How do you respond to this?

4. According to these verses, how has God made himself available to people?

5. In your experience today, would you describe God as being close or far away?

The Bottom Line

The vast universe points to a powerful and loving Creator. We can keep that Creator at a distance or we can seek ways to learn more about him. The choice is made easier by the fact that God desires for us to reach out and find him. He is not far from us!

Prayer

God, we stand in awe of your creation. Help this fact to make a difference in our lives. Amen.

A Final Word

The earth is the Lord's, and everything in it. *(David in Psalm 24:1)*

1: The Truth About God

Beginnings

As a youngster, how did you first visualize God? For example, was he a Santa Claus figure? A judge? A grandfather? How has your view of God changed as you've gotten older?

What's Happening Today

Some pollsters estimate that as many as 96 percent of North Americans claim to believe in God. People hold many different views of God, however. In fact, some of these views contradict each other.

To Marla, God was a loving grandfather type who would come to her aid when she called him. She didn't have much to do with God until she needed something or got into trouble, and then she would pray. Sometimes God seemed to answer and sometimes he did not. Marla would often become upset when everything did not go exactly as she had planned. As she grew older, she blamed God for what went wrong in her life.

Brad, on the other hand, patterned his idea of God after his own father, who was distant and selfish. Brad had a hard time praying to God, because he thought that the Creator of the universe, like his dad, probably had no interest in him. Brad always felt that he had to manage his own life, and he never thought to consult God in his daily decisions.

Carlos always felt guilty. He pictured God as a judge in a black robe. He believed that God either gave him the "thumbs up" or the "thumbs down" sign, depending on what he did. Usually it was "thumbs down," he figured. Carlos never considered himself good enough to please God, so could not believe that God would love him.

The Bible shows these impressions of God to be wrong. The following passages from the Bible paint a true portrait of God and show what he is really like.

What the Bible Tells Us

"To whom will you compare me?
Or who is my equal?" says the Holy One.
Lift your eyes and look to the heavens:
Who created all these?
He who brings out the starry host one by one,
*   and calls them each by name.*
Because of his great power and mighty strength,
*   not one of them is missing.* (Isaiah 40:25-26)

The God who made the world and everything in it is the Lord of heaven and earth and does not live in temples built by hands. And he is not served by human hands, as if he needed anything, because he himself gives all men life and breath and everything else. From one man he made every nation of men, that they should inhabit the whole earth; and he determined the times set for them and the exact places where they should live. God did this so that men would seek him and perhaps reach out for him and find him, though he is not far from each one of us. "For in him we live and move and have our being." (Acts 17:24-28)

How the Bible Relates

1. How did Isaiah react when he saw the night sky?

2. Can you recall a time when you were awed by the night sky as Isaiah was? What was your response?

3. What does the passage from Acts 17 presume about God in its opening statement? How do you respond to this?

4. According to these verses, how has God made himself available to people?

5. In your experience today, would you describe God as being close or far away?

The Bottom Line

The vast universe points to a powerful and loving Creator. We can keep that Creator at a distance or we can seek ways to learn more about him. The choice is made easier by the fact that God desires for us to reach out and find him. He is not far from us!

Prayer

God, we stand in awe of your creation. Help this fact to make a difference in our lives. Amen.

A Final Word

The earth is the Lord's, and everything in it. *(David in Psalm 24:1)*

1: The Truth About God

Beginnings

As a youngster, how did you first visualize God? For example, was he a Santa Claus figure? A judge? A grandfather? How has your view of God changed as you've gotten older?

What's Happening Today

Some pollsters estimate that as many as 96 percent of North Americans claim to believe in God. People hold many different views of God, however. In fact, some of these views contradict each other.

To Marla, God was a loving grandfather type who would come to her aid when she called him. She didn't have much to do with God until she needed something or got into trouble, and then she would pray. Sometimes God seemed to answer and sometimes he did not. Marla would often become upset when everything did not go exactly as she had planned. As she grew older, she blamed God for what went wrong in her life.

Brad, on the other hand, patterned his idea of God after his own father, who was distant and selfish. Brad had a hard time praying to God, because he thought that the Creator of the universe, like his dad, probably had no interest in him. Brad always felt that he had to manage his own life, and he never thought to consult God in his daily decisions.

Carlos always felt guilty. He pictured God as a judge in a black robe. He believed that God either gave him the "thumbs up" or the "thumbs down" sign, depending on what he did. Usually it was "thumbs down," he figured. Carlos never considered himself good enough to please God, so could not believe that God would love him.

The Bible shows these impressions of God to be wrong. The following passages from the Bible paint a true portrait of God and show what he is really like.

What the Bible Tells Us

"To whom will you compare me?
Or who is my equal?" says the Holy One.
Lift your eyes and look to the heavens:
Who created all these?
He who brings out the starry host one by one,
*   and calls them each by name.*
Because of his great power and mighty strength,
*   not one of them is missing. (Isaiah 40:25-26)*

The God who made the world and everything in it is the Lord of heaven and earth and does not live in temples built by hands. And he is not served by human hands, as if he needed anything, because he himself gives all men life and breath and everything else. From one man he made every nation of men, that they should inhabit the whole earth; and he determined the times set for them and the exact places where they should live. God did this so that men would seek him and perhaps reach out for him and find him, though he is not far from each one of us. "For in him we live and move and have our being." (Acts 17:24-28)

How the Bible Relates

1. How did Isaiah react when he saw the night sky?

2. Can you recall a time when you were awed by the night sky as Isaiah was? What was your response?

3. What does the passage from Acts 17 presume about God in its opening statement? How do you respond to this?

4. According to these verses, how has God made himself available to people?

5. In your experience today, would you describe God as being close or far away?

The Bottom Line

The vast universe points to a powerful and loving Creator. We can keep that Creator at a distance or we can seek ways to learn more about him. The choice is made easier by the fact that God desires for us to reach out and find him. He is not far from us!

Prayer

God, we stand in awe of your creation. Help this fact to make a difference in our lives. Amen.

A Final Word

The earth is the Lord's, and everything in it. *(David in Psalm 24:1)*

1: The Truth About God

Beginnings

As a youngster, how did you first visualize God? For example, was he a Santa Claus figure? A judge? A grandfather? How has your view of God changed as you've gotten older?

What's Happening Today

Some pollsters estimate that as many as 96 percent of North Americans claim to believe in God. People hold many different views of God, however. In fact, some of these views contradict each other.

To Marla, God was a loving grandfather type who would come to her aid when she called him. She didn't have much to do with God until she needed something or got into trouble, and then she would pray. Sometimes God seemed to answer and sometimes he did not. Marla would often become upset when everything did not go exactly as she had planned. As she grew older, she blamed God for what went wrong in her life.

Brad, on the other hand, patterned his idea of God after his own father, who was distant and selfish. Brad had a hard time praying to God, because he thought that the Creator of the universe, like his dad, probably had no interest in him. Brad always felt that he had to manage his own life, and he never thought to consult God in his daily decisions.

Carlos always felt guilty. He pictured God as a judge in a black robe. He believed that God either gave him the "thumbs up" or the "thumbs down" sign, depending on what he did. Usually it was "thumbs down," he figured. Carlos never considered himself good enough to please God, so could not believe that God would love him.

The Bible shows these impressions of God to be wrong. The following passages from the Bible paint a true portrait of God and show what he is really like.

What the Bible Tells Us

"To whom will you compare me?
Or who is my equal?" says the Holy One.
Lift your eyes and look to the heavens:
Who created all these?
He who brings out the starry host one by one,
*   and calls them each by name.*
Because of his great power and mighty strength,
*   not one of them is missing.* (Isaiah 40:25-26)

The God who made the world and everything in it is the Lord of heaven and earth and does not live in temples built by hands. And he is not served by human hands, as if he needed anything, because he himself gives all men life and breath and everything else. From one man he made every nation of men, that they should inhabit the whole earth; and he determined the times set for them and the exact places where they should live. God did this so that men would seek him and perhaps reach out for him and find him, though he is not far from each one of us. "For in him we live and move and have our being." (Acts 17:24-28)

How the Bible Relates

1. How did Isaiah react when he saw the night sky?

2. Can you recall a time when you were awed by the night sky as Isaiah was? What was your response?

3. What does the passage from Acts 17 presume about God in its opening statement? How do you respond to this?

4. According to these verses, how has God made himself available to people?

5. In your experience today, would you describe God as being close or far away?

The Bottom Line

The vast universe points to a powerful and loving Creator. We can keep that Creator at a distance or we can seek ways to learn more about him. The choice is made easier by the fact that God desires for us to reach out and find him. He is not far from us!

Prayer

God, we stand in awe of your creation. Help this fact to make a difference in our lives. Amen.

A Final Word

The earth is the Lord's, and everything in it. *(David in Psalm 24:1)*

1: The Truth About God

Beginnings

As a youngster, how did you first visualize God? For example, was he a Santa Claus figure? A judge? A grandfather? How has your view of God changed as you've gotten older?

What's Happening Today

Some pollsters estimate that as many as 96 percent of North Americans claim to believe in God. People hold many different views of God, however. In fact, some of these views contradict each other.

To Marla, God was a loving grandfather type who would come to her aid when she called him. She didn't have much to do with God until she needed something or got into trouble, and then she would pray. Sometimes God seemed to answer and sometimes he did not. Marla would often become upset when everything did not go exactly as she had planned. As she grew older, she blamed God for what went wrong in her life.

Brad, on the other hand, patterned his idea of God after his own father, who was distant and selfish. Brad had a hard time praying to God, because he thought that the Creator of the universe, like his dad, probably had no interest in him. Brad always felt that he had to manage his own life, and he never thought to consult God in his daily decisions.

Carlos always felt guilty. He pictured God as a judge in a black robe. He believed that God either gave him the "thumbs up" or the "thumbs down" sign, depending on what he did. Usually it was "thumbs down," he figured. Carlos never considered himself good enough to please God, so could not believe that God would love him.

The Bible shows these impressions of God to be wrong. The following passages from the Bible paint a true portrait of God and show what he is really like.

What the Bible Tells Us

"To whom will you compare me?
Or who is my equal?" says the Holy One.
Lift your eyes and look to the heavens:
Who created all these?
He who brings out the starry host one by one,
*   and calls them each by name.*
Because of his great power and mighty strength,
*   not one of them is missing.* (Isaiah 40:25-26)

The God who made the world and everything in it is the Lord of heaven and earth and does not live in temples built by hands. And he is not served by human hands, as if he needed anything, because he himself gives all men life and breath and everything else. From one man he made every nation of men, that they should inhabit the whole earth; and he determined the times set for them and the exact places where they should live. God did this so that men would seek him and perhaps reach out for him and find him, though he is not far from each one of us. "For in him we live and move and have our being." (Acts 17:24-28)

How the Bible Relates

1. How did Isaiah react when he saw the night sky?

2. Can you recall a time when you were awed by the night sky as Isaiah was? What was your response?

3. What does the passage from Acts 17 presume about God in its opening statement? How do you respond to this?

4. According to these verses, how has God made himself available to people?

5. In your experience today, would you describe God as being close or far away?

The Bottom Line

The vast universe points to a powerful and loving Creator. We can keep that Creator at a distance or we can seek ways to learn more about him. The choice is made easier by the fact that God desires for us to reach out and find him. He is not far from us!

Prayer

God, we stand in awe of your creation. Help this fact to make a difference in our lives. Amen.

A Final Word

The earth is the Lord's, and everything in it. *(David in Psalm 24:1)*

1: The Truth About God

Beginnings

As a youngster, how did you first visualize God? For example, was he a Santa Claus figure? A judge? A grandfather? How has your view of God changed as you've gotten older?

What's Happening Today

Some pollsters estimate that as many as 96 percent of North Americans claim to believe in God. People hold many different views of God, however. In fact, some of these views contradict each other.

To Marla, God was a loving grandfather type who would come to her aid when she called him. She didn't have much to do with God until she needed something or got into trouble, and then she would pray. Sometimes God seemed to answer and sometimes he did not. Marla would often become upset when everything did not go exactly as she had planned. As she grew older, she blamed God for what went wrong in her life.

Brad, on the other hand, patterned his idea of God after his own father, who was distant and selfish. Brad had a hard time praying to God, because he thought that the Creator of the universe, like his dad, probably had no interest in him. Brad always felt that he had to manage his own life, and he never thought to consult God in his daily decisions.

Carlos always felt guilty. He pictured God as a judge in a black robe. He believed that God either gave him the "thumbs up" or the "thumbs down" sign, depending on what he did. Usually it was "thumbs down," he figured. Carlos never considered himself good enough to please God, so could not believe that God would love him.

The Bible shows these impressions of God to be wrong. The following passages from the Bible paint a true portrait of God and show what he is really like.

What the Bible Tells Us

"To whom will you compare me?
Or who is my equal?" says the Holy One.
Lift your eyes and look to the heavens:
Who created all these?
He who brings out the starry host one by one,
*   and calls them each by name.*
Because of his great power and mighty strength,
*   not one of them is missing.* (Isaiah 40:25-26)

The God who made the world and everything in it is the Lord of heaven and earth and does not live in temples built by hands. And he is not served by human hands, as if he needed anything, because he himself gives all men life and breath and everything else. From one man he made every nation of men, that they should inhabit the whole earth; and he determined the times set for them and the exact places where they should live. God did this so that men would seek him and perhaps reach out for him and find him, though he is not far from each one of us. "For in him we live and move and have our being." (Acts 17:24-28)

How the Bible Relates

1. How did Isaiah react when he saw the night sky?

2. Can you recall a time when you were awed by the night sky as Isaiah was? What was your response?

3. What does the passage from Acts 17 presume about God in its opening statement? How do you respond to this?

4. According to these verses, how has God made himself available to people?

5. In your experience today, would you describe God as being close or far away?

The Bottom Line

The vast universe points to a powerful and loving Creator. We can keep that Creator at a distance or we can seek ways to learn more about him. The choice is made easier by the fact that God desires for us to reach out and find him. He is not far from us!

Prayer

God, we stand in awe of your creation. Help this fact to make a difference in our lives. Amen.

A Final Word

The earth is the Lord's, and everything in it. *(David in Psalm 24:1)*

The Whole Truth and Nothing But the Truth

2: The Truth About the Bible

Introductory Notes

This exciting study deals with the book that is different from any other. Your group members will meet Jesus, the living Word, on the pages of the printed Word. In this book they can find new life. Pray that your discussion today will open their eyes to the truth of Scripture and will whet their appetite to read it on their own.

As you prepare for this session, consider how the Bible has been a living force in your life. How have you found it useful "for teaching, rebuking, correcting, and training in righteousness"? How has it "equipped you for every good work"? The more you actively use the Bible, the better you will be able to communicate the truth of the passages chosen for this session. Have you allowed this Word to shape your own life—even when it meant painful change?

Remember, as Hebrews says, "the word of God is living and active." It will be a powerful force for good in your group members' lives. Through the activity of the Holy Spirit, it will affect their attitude toward life, their behavior, and their relationships with others and God.

The Bible may also confront them with their greatest fears and weaknesses: "Sharper than any double-edged sword, it penetrates even to dividing soul and spirit . . .; it judges the thoughts and attitudes of the heart" (Hebrews 4:12). For that reason, some may draw back from it at first. But keep praying for them; they are showing signs of the Spirit at work.

Remember, too, that most people do not understand the power of the Scriptures. Acknowledging that the Bible is a unique book requires a step of faith. Your group members may not readily accept that, through human writers, God gave us this book.

You cannot convince anybody of this by logical argument; God's Spirit must work from beginning to end. They must experience the power. Pray that God will open their eyes to the wonder of this book.

Beginning the Session

Greet the members warmly and personally as they gather for this session. This is an ideal time to follow up on any needs or concerns they expressed at the end of the last session. Mentally note any special needs that members might mention; be sure to include these in your prayer time at the end.

This is a good session to make sure that everyone has a Bible. (You can purchase them inexpensively through organizations such as Gideons International, the American Bible Society, or the Bible League. Perhaps a church in your area would donate some Bibles to your group.) If possible, give members the same easy-to-read translation.

Distribute the discussion handouts and make sure everyone has a pen or pencil and is comfortably seated before you ask the "Beginnings" questions to start the session.

Beginnings

What kinds of books—both religious and nonreligious—determine how people live? What religious books—old or new—do people read and use today? Have you ever read any of them, including the Bible? Do you think that the Bible is different from any of these books? Why or why not?

Keep these first questions open-ended. Some in your group may be exploring the spiritual side of life for the first time. Give them the freedom to share which books have influenced their lives, even if they are not religious. Their responses will help you better understand their point of view.

Whether or not they realize it, people pattern their lives on what they read. **What might business people read as their "Bible"? What about those whose self-esteem is wrapped up in their appearance or in attracting the opposite sex?** For some it may be the *Wall Street Journal*, for others a romance novel or supermarket tabloid. Still others take their cues from the horoscope in the newspaper or Dr. Spock's book on child rearing. Some look for books with strong spiritual themes and explore religious writings. Scores of such books—from ancient Buddhism to New Age thinking—are sold today.

Find out what group members have read. Ask questions that help them summarize briefly what they remember, but avoid lengthy discussions that can drive you off track. Always steer your discussion back to comparison with the Bible: **What claims do these books make for themselves? Who are the authors? What effect might these writings have on a person's life?** Don't go too deeply into this; simply use these questions to get your group thinking.

 In the extended format, you may want to bring along some copies of books on spirituality—particularly if you can use them for comparison in this session. Pass them around for members to leaf through. Be prepared to answer questions during the session (especially later, as you discuss the study questions) as to how the Bible is different from all these books.

What's Happening Today

Read this section aloud to your group. Tie it to your discussion of the "Beginnings" question and use it to introduce the Bible passages that follow.

What the Bible Tells Us

Unless one or two group members volunteer to read this section to the group, read it aloud yourself. Do so slowly and expressively enough so that the words have their greatest impact.

Members may have some trouble understanding some of the terms in these Scriptures. Here are a few you may want to help clarify:

Scripture—another word for the Bible

prophecy—a message from God that is given to one person (a prophet) to be shared with everyone

Holy Spirit—the Spirit of God

If nobody has further questions regarding the meaning of words, move on to the discussion questions.

How the Bible Relates

1. Where did the prophecies, or messages, of Scripture come from?

The Scriptures did not originate from the writers' own thoughts or will—this is the first quality that sets the Scriptures apart from other religious writings. Make sure members grasp what the passage says. Be sure to clarify the more difficult terms mentioned above, especially "prophecy."

Draw the meaning of "prophecy" from group members. **Does anyone know what it means?** Look up the definition in the dictionary, if one is available. Help members to understand that "prophecy" refers to a message or special revelation of knowledge given to someone by God. That message is intended to be communicated to a larger group of people. This is one of the ways that God communicates with people.

In the past, many of these prophecies were written down, and they form a large part of the Bible, which also includes poetry, history, prayers and songs, and letters to early churches. These, along with the major and minor prophetic books, form the entire collection of books that comprise the Scripture.

 In the extended format, you may want to leaf through the Bible with your group members, pointing out various kinds of books found in its pages. Point out some of your favorite books and encourage them to explore the Scriptures more broadly on their own. Ask if any of them have a particular part of the Bible or Bible verse that they are interested in or curious about. Take a few moments to talk about when or where they became aware of that portion of the Bible and why it interests them.

You also might take the time to look at a few of the major prophetic books in the Bible. Isaiah 2:1-5 is a beautiful prophecy, as are Isaiah 8:14 and 53:1-6, Ezekiel 11:16-20, and Revelation 21:1-5. 1 Peter 1:10-12 also casts an interesting light on the prophecies concerning Jesus Christ. Don't spend too much time on these passages, but use them to increase members' interest in reading the Bible for themselves.

Listen closely to what your group members say. Ask questions to find out more about where they're coming from. **What did you think of the Bible before beginning this study? Have you ever thought of the Bible as being a book written by God? Does that make it different from other religious books? Why or why not?** Don't attempt to argue a point; emphasize that you're merely looking at what the Bible says and letting it speak for itself.

Look also at the process that this passage describes. **Who were the Scripture writers speaking for or from? Who "carried them along"? What do you think this means? How could this process still preserve the individual styles and personalities of those who wrote the various books?** Note that authors' writing styles are often shaped by their personalities and the events happening when they wrote. In spite of this, the Bible's unity of teaching and perspective is amazing, given the many writers and different eras in which they wrote.

2. What picture comes to mind when it says Scripture is "God-breathed"? What do you think this means?

As you look together at the passage from 2 Timothy, you may want to mention ways in which other versions of the Bible have translated the phrase "God-breathed": "given by God" (New Century Version), "inspired by God" (Revised Standard Version), "given to us by inspiration from God" (*The Living Bible*). **What idea is common in all of these expressions? What role did God play in writing the Bible? In what sense can we say that it has been given to us directly from God? How does this relate to the statement in 2 Peter that the writers were "carried along by the Holy Spirit"?**

The words "God-breathed" are particularly descriptive. Christians familiar with the Bible will think of creation when "the Lord God . . . breathed into the man's nostrils the breath of life, and the man became a living being" (Genesis 2:7). The Holy Spirit also is often referred to as "breath" or "wind" in the New Testament. Newcomers to Bible study will probably have no knowledge of this, but look with them at the picture of God's breathing into this book a spiritual power and life that no other book has. **What does the word "breathe" convey to you?** Hopefully the group will see its life-giving component. What the Scriptures have power to do is explained more fully in the next few questions.

Touch on one more point: the authority of the Scriptures. **If God has given them to us, as the Scriptures** claim, what importance should they have in one's life? How much weight should a person give to them? How important is it to read the Scripture and know what it says? Listen carefully to group members' responses as they reveal their viewpoints. People in North American society have a hard time acknowledging an authority higher than themselves (other than perhaps the government or their employer). They have grown up with the concept that individuals take responsibility for their own lives and are free to live as they wish, as long as their lifestyle does not harm someone else. The Bible's claim to be God-breathed may not be easy to accept, since it places the Scripture in a position of authority.

Do not try to argue group members into accepting the Bible's God-given authority. Make sure, however, that they understand that if the Bible truly comes from God, then it has the authority that it claims to have. As such, it is worth studying and obeying. Pray that God will open their eyes and nurture the seeds of faith that are being planted in members' hearts through this discussion.

3. For what is Scripture useful?

Look at each of these items separately: teaching, rebuking, correcting, and training. According to this passage, God intends the Scriptures first of all to teach people. **What might God want to teach people about himself? About their lifestyles? About their relationship to God and to others?**

Help group members see that the Bible contains a wealth of information that teaches us who God is and what role God wants to play in our lives. It teaches us who we are, where we come from, and what our purpose is in life. It also helps us deal with problems in relationships, in finances, in our lifestyle choices. In other words, it is the ultimate source of wisdom and insight that answers any person's deepest questions.

The word "rebuking" can carry harsh overtones, but the New Century Version translates it this way: "showing people what is wrong in their lives." **Why do we need this in our society? What evidence in the daily news; in television programs and movies; and in the crowded courts, prisons, and psychiatrists' offices shows that something is wrong in people's lives? How might these problems be connected to people's relationship (or lack of relationship) to God?** Again, listen closely as your group discusses these questions. Learn what group members think, and let them come to their own conclusion that there certainly is a need today for "showing people what is wrong in their lives"—and that the Bible may be the best place to start looking for that guidance.

Why isn't simply showing someone what's wrong enough? A person in the wrong must be shown what is right. They need to be corrected and trained in righteousness (or, as the New Century Version puts it, "taught how to live right"). **How does "correcting" take us one step further?**

 In the extended format, ask if group members are familiar with any guidelines in the Scriptures that are meant to correct the things that are wrong in our lives. Some may mention the Ten Commandments or the Golden Rule. Others will not know the Bible well enough to suggest anything here. If so, you might want to read a few of the Ten Commandments, especially the last five. **How might following these guidelines correct the wrong in our world? How do they teach people how to live right?**

Be sure that group members understand that "righteousness" means simply "living right." Or, to look at it from another perspective, it means having a clean record with God—living completely the way God approves of.

4. What does it equip people to do?

Ask group members to imagine that they have been hired for a high-level, powerful job in a highly specialized profession. They have told the boss that they are not fully qualified, but he hires them anyway. Now they show up for work the first day, expecting at least two or three weeks of training before they take over the position. Instead, what they find is an empty office and a sign that says, "Get to work! We want results!"

Facing a difficult task without proper training is frightening. **What does the Scripture promise? If a person reads it faithfully, what will he or she receive? How well equipped will that person be?** Note the word "thoroughly" and the assurance that it brings to the one who has been trained.

What seems to be the task that the man or woman of God will be asked to face? "Every good work" seems a daunting task—if not impossible. And yet it's the highest goal that any of us can work toward. Help your group to see that God does not intend us to work mainly to get ahead as individuals, for the benefit of our own careers or lifestyles. That goal in life leads to emptiness and disillusionment, as many in our society have learned.

 In the extended format you may want to explore this further with the following questions: **Why is it so easy to fall into the trap of thinking that our main goal is "looking out for Number One"? Do you know anyone personally who has experienced the emptiness of living only for self? Who in the news lately might provide a good example of this?** Listen closely as group members share their insights here. The more they are able to connect the Bible passages with their own experiences, the more likely they are to see it as a book that is relevant and important to their lives.

Note that the full, meaningful life that God intended for us is one of doing good for others as well as for ourselves. As Ephesians 2:10 says, "In Christ Jesus, God made us new people so that we would do good works. God had planned in advance those good works for us. He had planned for us to live our lives doing them" (New Century Version). **How would you define "good works"? How do they benefit the person doing them? How do they benefit the person on the receiving end?**

Reaffirm that the Bible is the most important resource we have in learning how to live the kind of life God intended.

5. Why might it be worthwhile to read the Bible?

Use this question first of all to learn what your group members have been learning and thinking throughout this session. **What makes the Scripture seem valuable or useful, according to the passages we read today? How might it help you deal with some tough situations in your life? Would you like to learn more about God? Why or why not? If there's a chance that this book, the Bible, has actually been given to us by God, would that make you want to read it carefully to find out for yourself what it says?**

Obviously the members of your group, having agreed to participate in this discussion, already have some interest in the Bible. Help them to put into words some of their curiosity or fascination with the Scripture. Verbalizing it with others will help make it more real and specific for them.

Also use this question to share briefly what the Bible means in your own life. Be as specific as possible, showing where you found correction for some areas of weakness or wrong thinking and behavior in your own life and relationships. Mention a time when the Scripture equipped you to do something good that you thought was impossible—or at least extremely difficult—before you tried it.

Do your best to end this session by leaving group members with the impression that there is a power—a God-breathed, life-changing power—in the Scriptures. And, as you lead the discussion, remember always to make love and respect your first aim—because, as someone once said, you may be the only Bible that some people read.

Let group members see the love and power of God in your life, and they will be much more likely to open the written Word as well, on your suggestion. Yes, this is a high goal to attain. But you will find in your own study of God's Word the resources to fully equip you for this task!

The Bottom Line

The Bible claims that it was written by the inspiration of God the Holy Spirit. This alone makes it different from any other book in the world—and worth studying. Since its power can change lives, correct faults, and equip people for doing good, we need to seriously consider this book.

Read this paragraph to your group as a way of summing up the insights and Scriptures you've discussed today. If time allows, give members a chance to reflect on and respond to this statement.

Optional Prayer Time

As you pray this prayer with your group, you may want to add your own prayer for the people who are studying with you, asking God to open their eyes to what he may have to say to each individual through his Word. Also include in your prayer any special needs that you are aware of within the group. When you've finished your prayer, be sure to follow up on those needs by offering any kind of practical assistance and support that you can.

Prayer

Dear God, help me to read and understand this book, the Bible. If it is truly from you, show me your power by changing my life through what I read. Amen.

A Final Word

God's word is alive and working. It is sharper than a sword sharpened on both sides. It cuts all the way into us, where the soul and the spirit are joined. It cuts to the center of our joints and our bones. And God's word judges the thoughts and feelings in our hearts. Nothing in all the world can be hidden from God. Everything is clear and lies open before him. *(The writer of Hebrews in Hebrews 4:12, New Century Version)*

2: The Truth About the Bible

Beginnings

What kinds of books—both religious and nonreligious—determine how people live? What religious books—old or new—do people read and use today? Have you ever read any of them, including the Bible? Do you think that the Bible is different from any of these books? Why or why not?

What's Happening Today

In November 1994, *Newsweek* came out with a powerful cover story: "In Search of the Sacred." Recent polls of North American society show that "millions of Americans are embarking on a search for the sacred in their lives. . . . The seekers fit no particular profile. They include Wall Street investment bankers who spend their lunch hours in Bible study groups, artists rediscovering religious themes, fitness addicts who have traded aerobics classes for meditation and other spiritual exercises. No matter what path they take, the seekers are united by a sincere desire to find answers to proud questions, to understand their place in the cosmos."

Newsweek notes the number of books appearing on the subject of religion: "What distinguishes the current generation of self-help literature is the author's use of frankly religious language. Words like 'soul,' 'sacred,' 'spiritual' and 'sacramental' turn up regularly in today's best-selling guidebooks."

Bookstore shelves are lined with authors from all sorts of religious persuasions. New Age mixes with Christian and Buddhist literature. Even psychology now adds the perspective of religion and spirituality to self-help books.

Such an array can be confusing enough. Add to that the "sacred" books of the world's major religions—the Bible, the Koran, the Book of Mormon, the sayings of Buddha, and many others—and people's search for meaning can take many paths.

One of these "sacred" books differs from all the others. It makes unique claims, and it points to a God who is different from those of any other religion.

What book is that? What makes it different? The passages that follow identify that sacred book as the Bible. Learn what the Bible has to say about itself.

What the Bible Tells Us

Above all, you must understand that no prophecy of Scripture came about by the prophet's own interpretation. For prophecy never had its origin in the will of man, but men spoke from God as they were carried along by the Holy Spirit. (2 Peter 1:20-21)

All Scripture is God-breathed and is useful for teaching, rebuking, correcting and training in righteousness, so that the man of God may be thoroughly equipped for every good work. (2 Timothy 3:16-17)

How the Bible Relates

1. Where did the prophecies, or messages, of Scripture come from?

2. What picture comes to mind when it says Scripture is "God-breathed"? What do you think this means?

3. For what is Scripture useful?

4. What does it equip people to do?

5. Why might it be worthwhile to read the Bible?

The Bottom Line

The Bible claims that it was written by the inspiration of God the Holy Spirit. This alone makes it different from any other book in the world—and worth studying. Since its power can change lives, correct faults, and equip people for doing good, we need to seriously consider this book.

Prayer

Dear God, help me to read and understand this book, the Bible. If it is truly from you, show me your power by changing my life through what I read. Amen.

A Final Word

God's word is alive and working. It is sharper than a sword sharpened on both sides. It cuts all the way into us, where the soul and the spirit are joined. It cuts to the center of our joints and our bones. And God's word judges the thoughts and feelings in our hearts. Nothing in all the world can be hidden from God. Everything is clear and lies open before him. *(The writer of Hebrews in Hebrews 4:12, New Century Version)*

2: The Truth About the Bible

Beginnings

What kinds of books—both religious and nonreligious—determine how people live? What religious books—old or new—do people read and use today? Have you ever read any of them, including the Bible? Do you think that the Bible is different from any of these books? Why or why not?

What's Happening Today

In November 1994, *Newsweek* came out with a powerful cover story: "In Search of the Sacred." Recent polls of North American society show that "millions of Americans are embarking on a search for the sacred in their lives.... The seekers fit no particular profile. They include Wall Street investment bankers who spend their lunch hours in Bible study groups, artists rediscovering religious themes, fitness addicts who have traded aerobics classes for meditation and other spiritual exercises. No matter what path they take, the seekers are united by a sincere desire to find answers to proud questions, to understand their place in the cosmos."

Newsweek notes the number of books appearing on the subject of religion: "What distinguishes the current generation of self-help literature is the author's use of frankly religious language. Words like 'soul,' 'sacred,' 'spiritual' and 'sacramental' turn up regularly in today's best-selling guidebooks."

Bookstore shelves are lined with authors from all sorts of religious persuasions. New Age mixes with Christian and Buddhist literature. Even psychology now adds the perspective of religion and spirituality to self-help books.

Such an array can be confusing enough. Add to that the "sacred" books of the world's major religions—the Bible, the Koran, the Book of Mormon, the sayings of Buddha, and many others—and people's search for meaning can take many paths.

One of these "sacred" books differs from all the others. It makes unique claims, and it points to a God who is different from those of any other religion.

What book is that? What makes it different? The passages that follow identify that sacred book as the Bible. Learn what the Bible has to say about itself.

What the Bible Tells Us

Above all, you must understand that no prophecy of Scripture came about by the prophet's own interpretation. For prophecy never had its origin in the will of man, but men spoke from God as they were carried along by the Holy Spirit. (2 Peter 1:20-21)

All Scripture is God-breathed and is useful for teaching, rebuking, correcting and training in righteousness, so that the man of God may be thoroughly equipped for every good work. (2 Timothy 3:16-17)

How the Bible Relates

1. Where did the prophecies, or messages, of Scripture come from?

2. What picture comes to mind when it says Scripture is "God-breathed"? What do you think this means?

3. For what is Scripture useful?

4. What does it equip people to do?

5. Why might it be worthwhile to read the Bible?

The Bottom Line

The Bible claims that it was written by the inspiration of God the Holy Spirit. This alone makes it different from any other book in the world—and worth studying. Since its power can change lives, correct faults, and equip people for doing good, we need to seriously consider this book.

Prayer

Dear God, help me to read and understand this book, the Bible. If it is truly from you, show me your power by changing my life through what I read. Amen.

A Final Word

God's word is alive and working. It is sharper than a sword sharpened on both sides. It cuts all the way into us, where the soul and the spirit are joined. It cuts to the center of our joints and our bones. And God's word judges the thoughts and feelings in our hearts. Nothing in all the world can be hidden from God. Everything is clear and lies open before him. *(The writer of Hebrews in Hebrews 4:12, New Century Version)*

2: The Truth About the Bible

Beginnings

What kinds of books—both religious and nonreligious—determine how people live? What religious books—old or new—do people read and use today? Have you ever read any of them, including the Bible? Do you think that the Bible is different from any of these books? Why or why not?

What's Happening Today

In November 1994, *Newsweek* came out with a powerful cover story: "In Search of the Sacred." Recent polls of North American society show that "millions of Americans are embarking on a search for the sacred in their lives. . . . The seekers fit no particular profile. They include Wall Street investment bankers who spend their lunch hours in Bible study groups, artists rediscovering religious themes, fitness addicts who have traded aerobics classes for meditation and other spiritual exercises. No matter what path they take, the seekers are united by a sincere desire to find answers to proud questions, to understand their place in the cosmos."

Newsweek notes the number of books appearing on the subject of religion: "What distinguishes the current generation of self-help literature is the author's use of frankly religious language. Words like 'soul,' 'sacred,' 'spiritual' and 'sacramental' turn up regularly in today's best-selling guidebooks."

Bookstore shelves are lined with authors from all sorts of religious persuasions. New Age mixes with Christian and Buddhist literature. Even psychology now adds the perspective of religion and spirituality to self-help books.

Such an array can be confusing enough. Add to that the "sacred" books of the world's major religions—the Bible, the Koran, the Book of Mormon, the sayings of Buddha, and many others—and people's search for meaning can take many paths.

One of these "sacred" books differs from all the others. It makes unique claims, and it points to a God who is different from those of any other religion.

What book is that? What makes it different? The passages that follow identify that sacred book as the Bible. Learn what the Bible has to say about itself.

What the Bible Tells Us

Above all, you must understand that no prophecy of Scripture came about by the prophet's own interpretation. For prophecy never had its origin in the will of man, but men spoke from God as they were carried along by the Holy Spirit. (2 Peter 1:20-21)

All Scripture is God-breathed and is useful for teaching, rebuking, correcting and training in righteousness, so that the man of God may be thoroughly equipped for every good work. (2 Timothy 3:16-17)

How the Bible Relates

1. Where did the prophecies, or messages, of Scripture come from?

2. What picture comes to mind when it says Scripture is "God-breathed"? What do you think this means?

3. For what is Scripture useful?

4. What does it equip people to do?

5. Why might it be worthwhile to read the Bible?

The Bottom Line

The Bible claims that it was written by the inspiration of God the Holy Spirit. This alone makes it different from any other book in the world—and worth studying. Since its power can change lives, correct faults, and equip people for doing good, we need to seriously consider this book.

Prayer

Dear God, help me to read and understand this book, the Bible. If it is truly from you, show me your power by changing my life through what I read. Amen.

A Final Word

God's word is alive and working. It is sharper than a sword sharpened on both sides. It cuts all the way into us, where the soul and the spirit are joined. It cuts to the center of our joints and our bones. And God's word judges the thoughts and feelings in our hearts. Nothing in all the world can be hidden from God. Everything is clear and lies open before him. *(The writer of Hebrews in Hebrews 4:12, New Century Version)*

2: The Truth About the Bible

Beginnings

What kinds of books—both religious and nonreligious—determine how people live? What religious books—old or new—do people read and use today? Have you ever read any of them, including the Bible? Do you think that the Bible is different from any of these books? Why or why not?

What's Happening Today

In November 1994, *Newsweek* came out with a powerful cover story: "In Search of the Sacred." Recent polls of North American society show that "millions of Americans are embarking on a search for the sacred in their lives. . . . The seekers fit no particular profile. They include Wall Street investment bankers who spend their lunch hours in Bible study groups, artists rediscovering religious themes, fitness addicts who have traded aerobics classes for meditation and other spiritual exercises. No matter what path they take, the seekers are united by a sincere desire to find answers to proud questions, to understand their place in the cosmos."

Newsweek notes the number of books appearing on the subject of religion: "What distinguishes the current generation of self-help literature is the author's use of frankly religious language. Words like 'soul,' 'sacred,' 'spiritual' and 'sacramental' turn up regularly in today's best-selling guidebooks."

Bookstore shelves are lined with authors from all sorts of religious persuasions. New Age mixes with Christian and Buddhist literature. Even psychology now adds the perspective of religion and spirituality to self-help books.

Such an array can be confusing enough. Add to that the "sacred" books of the world's major religions—the Bible, the Koran, the Book of Mormon, the sayings of Buddha, and many others—and people's search for meaning can take many paths.

One of these "sacred" books differs from all the others. It makes unique claims, and it points to a God who is different from those of any other religion.

What book is that? What makes it different? The passages that follow identify that sacred book as the Bible. Learn what the Bible has to say about itself.

What the Bible Tells Us

Above all, you must understand that no prophecy of Scripture came about by the prophet's own interpretation. For prophecy never had its origin in the will of man, but men spoke from God as they were carried along by the Holy Spirit. (2 Peter 1:20-21)

All Scripture is God-breathed and is useful for teaching, rebuking, correcting and training in righteousness, so that the man of God may be thoroughly equipped for every good work. (2 Timothy 3:16-17)

How the Bible Relates

1. Where did the prophecies, or messages, of Scripture come from?

2. What picture comes to mind when it says Scripture is "God-breathed"? What do you think this means?

3. For what is Scripture useful?

4. What does it equip people to do?

5. Why might it be worthwhile to read the Bible?

The Bottom Line

The Bible claims that it was written by the inspiration of God the Holy Spirit. This alone makes it different from any other book in the world—and worth studying. Since its power can change lives, correct faults, and equip people for doing good, we need to seriously consider this book.

Prayer

Dear God, help me to read and understand this book, the Bible. If it is truly from you, show me your power by changing my life through what I read. Amen.

A Final Word

God's word is alive and working. It is sharper than a sword sharpened on both sides. It cuts all the way into us, where the soul and the spirit are joined. It cuts to the center of our joints and our bones. And God's word judges the thoughts and feelings in our hearts. Nothing in all the world can be hidden from God. Everything is clear and lies open before him. *(The writer of Hebrews in Hebrews 4:12, New Century Version)*

2: The Truth About the Bible

Beginnings

What kinds of books—both religious and nonreligious—determine how people live? What religious books—old or new—do people read and use today? Have you ever read any of them, including the Bible? Do you think that the Bible is different from any of these books? Why or why not?

What's Happening Today

In November 1994, *Newsweek* came out with a powerful cover story: "In Search of the Sacred." Recent polls of North American society show that "millions of Americans are embarking on a search for the sacred in their lives. . . . The seekers fit no particular profile. They include Wall Street investment bankers who spend their lunch hours in Bible study groups, artists rediscovering religious themes, fitness addicts who have traded aerobics classes for meditation and other spiritual exercises. No matter what path they take, the seekers are united by a sincere desire to find answers to proud questions, to understand their place in the cosmos."

Newsweek notes the number of books appearing on the subject of religion: "What distinguishes the current generation of self-help literature is the author's use of frankly religious language. Words like 'soul,' 'sacred,' 'spiritual' and 'sacramental' turn up regularly in today's best-selling guidebooks."

Bookstore shelves are lined with authors from all sorts of religious persuasions. New Age mixes with Christian and Buddhist literature. Even psychology now adds the perspective of religion and spirituality to self-help books.

Such an array can be confusing enough. Add to that the "sacred" books of the world's major religions—the Bible, the Koran, the Book of Mormon, the sayings of Buddha, and many others—and people's search for meaning can take many paths.

One of these "sacred" books differs from all the others. It makes unique claims, and it points to a God who is different from those of any other religion.

What book is that? What makes it different? The passages that follow identify that sacred book as the Bible. Learn what the Bible has to say about itself.

What the Bible Tells Us

Above all, you must understand that no prophecy of Scripture came about by the prophet's own interpretation. For prophecy never had its origin in the will of man, but men spoke from God as they were carried along by the Holy Spirit. (2 Peter 1:20-21)

All Scripture is God-breathed and is useful for teaching, rebuking, correcting and training in righteousness, so that the man of God may be thoroughly equipped for every good work. (2 Timothy 3:16-17)

How the Bible Relates

1. Where did the prophecies, or messages, of Scripture come from?

2. What picture comes to mind when it says Scripture is "God-breathed"? What do you think this means?

3. For what is Scripture useful?

4. What does it equip people to do?

5. Why might it be worthwhile to read the Bible?

The Bottom Line

The Bible claims that it was written by the inspiration of God the Holy Spirit. This alone makes it different from any other book in the world—and worth studying. Since its power can change lives, correct faults, and equip people for doing good, we need to seriously consider this book.

Prayer

Dear God, help me to read and understand this book, the Bible. If it is truly from you, show me your power by changing my life through what I read. Amen.

A Final Word

God's word is alive and working. It is sharper than a sword sharpened on both sides. It cuts all the way into us, where the soul and the spirit are joined. It cuts to the center of our joints and our bones. And God's word judges the thoughts and feelings in our hearts. Nothing in all the world can be hidden from God. Everything is clear and lies open before him. *(The writer of Hebrews in Hebrews 4:12, New Century Version)*

2: The Truth About the Bible

Beginnings

What kinds of books—both religious and nonreligious—determine how people live? What religious books—old or new—do people read and use today? Have you ever read any of them, including the Bible? Do you think that the Bible is different from any of these books? Why or why not?

What's Happening Today

In November 1994, *Newsweek* came out with a powerful cover story: "In Search of the Sacred." Recent polls of North American society show that "millions of Americans are embarking on a search for the sacred in their lives. . . . The seekers fit no particular profile. They include Wall Street investment bankers who spend their lunch hours in Bible study groups, artists rediscovering religious themes, fitness addicts who have traded aerobics classes for meditation and other spiritual exercises. No matter what path they take, the seekers are united by a sincere desire to find answers to proud questions, to understand their place in the cosmos."

Newsweek notes the number of books appearing on the subject of religion: "What distinguishes the current generation of self-help literature is the author's use of frankly religious language. Words like 'soul,' 'sacred,' 'spiritual' and 'sacramental' turn up regularly in today's best-selling guidebooks."

Bookstore shelves are lined with authors from all sorts of religious persuasions. New Age mixes with Christian and Buddhist literature. Even psychology now adds the perspective of religion and spirituality to self-help books.

Such an array can be confusing enough. Add to that the "sacred" books of the world's major religions—the Bible, the Koran, the Book of Mormon, the sayings of Buddha, and many others—and people's search for meaning can take many paths.

One of these "sacred" books differs from all the others. It makes unique claims, and it points to a God who is different from those of any other religion.

What book is that? What makes it different? The passages that follow identify that sacred book as the Bible. Learn what the Bible has to say about itself.

What the Bible Tells Us

Above all, you must understand that no prophecy of Scripture came about by the prophet's own interpretation. For prophecy never had its origin in the will of man, but men spoke from God as they were carried along by the Holy Spirit. (2 Peter 1:20-21)

All Scripture is God-breathed and is useful for teaching, rebuking, correcting and training in righteousness, so that the man of God may be thoroughly equipped for every good work. (2 Timothy 3:16-17)

How the Bible Relates

1. Where did the prophecies, or messages, of Scripture come from?

2. What picture comes to mind when it says Scripture is "God-breathed"? What do you think this means?

3. For what is Scripture useful?

4. What does it equip people to do?

5. Why might it be worthwhile to read the Bible?

The Bottom Line

The Bible claims that it was written by the inspiration of God the Holy Spirit. This alone makes it different from any other book in the world—and worth studying. Since its power can change lives, correct faults, and equip people for doing good, we need to seriously consider this book.

Prayer

Dear God, help me to read and understand this book, the Bible. If it is truly from you, show me your power by changing my life through what I read. Amen.

A Final Word

God's word is alive and working. It is sharper than a sword sharpened on both sides. It cuts all the way into us, where the soul and the spirit are joined. It cuts to the center of our joints and our bones. And God's word judges the thoughts and feelings in our hearts. Nothing in all the world can be hidden from God. Everything is clear and lies open before him. *(The writer of Hebrews in Hebrews 4:12, New Century Version)*

2: The Truth About the Bible

Beginnings

What kinds of books—both religious and nonreligious—determine how people live? What religious books—old or new—do people read and use today? Have you ever read any of them, including the Bible? Do you think that the Bible is different from any of these books? Why or why not?

What's Happening Today

In November 1994, *Newsweek* came out with a powerful cover story: "In Search of the Sacred." Recent polls of North American society show that "millions of Americans are embarking on a search for the sacred in their lives. . . . The seekers fit no particular profile. They include Wall Street investment bankers who spend their lunch hours in Bible study groups, artists rediscovering religious themes, fitness addicts who have traded aerobics classes for meditation and other spiritual exercises. No matter what path they take, the seekers are united by a sincere desire to find answers to proud questions, to understand their place in the cosmos."

Newsweek notes the number of books appearing on the subject of religion: "What distinguishes the current generation of self-help literature is the author's use of frankly religious language. Words like 'soul,' 'sacred,' 'spiritual' and 'sacramental' turn up regularly in today's best-selling guidebooks."

Bookstore shelves are lined with authors from all sorts of religious persuasions. New Age mixes with Christian and Buddhist literature. Even psychology now adds the perspective of religion and spirituality to self-help books.

Such an array can be confusing enough. Add to that the "sacred" books of the world's major religions—the Bible, the Koran, the Book of Mormon, the sayings of Buddha, and many others—and people's search for meaning can take many paths.

One of these "sacred" books differs from all the others. It makes unique claims, and it points to a God who is different from those of any other religion.

What book is that? What makes it different? The passages that follow identify that sacred book as the Bible. Learn what the Bible has to say about itself.

What the Bible Tells Us

Above all, you must understand that no prophecy of Scripture came about by the prophet's own interpretation. For prophecy never had its origin in the will of man, but men spoke from God as they were carried along by the Holy Spirit. (2 Peter 1:20-21)

All Scripture is God-breathed and is useful for teaching, rebuking, correcting and training in righteousness, so that the man of God may be thoroughly equipped for every good work. (2 Timothy 3:16-17)

How the Bible Relates

1. Where did the prophecies, or messages, of Scripture come from?

2. What picture comes to mind when it says Scripture is "God-breathed"? What do you think this means?

3. For what is Scripture useful?

4. What does it equip people to do?

5. Why might it be worthwhile to read the Bible?

The Bottom Line

The Bible claims that it was written by the inspiration of God the Holy Spirit. This alone makes it different from any other book in the world—and worth studying. Since its power can change lives, correct faults, and equip people for doing good, we need to seriously consider this book.

Prayer

Dear God, help me to read and understand this book, the Bible. If it is truly from you, show me your power by changing my life through what I read. Amen.

A Final Word

God's word is alive and working. It is sharper than a sword sharpened on both sides. It cuts all the way into us, where the soul and the spirit are joined. It cuts to the center of our joints and our bones. And God's word judges the thoughts and feelings in our hearts. Nothing in all the world can be hidden from God. Everything is clear and lies open before him. *(The writer of Hebrews in Hebrews 4:12, New Century Version)*

2: The Truth About the Bible

Beginnings

What kinds of books—both religious and nonreligious—determine how people live? What religious books—old or new—do people read and use today? Have you ever read any of them, including the Bible? Do you think that the Bible is different from any of these books? Why or why not?

What's Happening Today

In November 1994, *Newsweek* came out with a powerful cover story: "In Search of the Sacred." Recent polls of North American society show that "millions of Americans are embarking on a search for the sacred in their lives. . . . The seekers fit no particular profile. They include Wall Street investment bankers who spend their lunch hours in Bible study groups, artists rediscovering religious themes, fitness addicts who have traded aerobics classes for meditation and other spiritual exercises. No matter what path they take, the seekers are united by a sincere desire to find answers to proud questions, to understand their place in the cosmos."

Newsweek notes the number of books appearing on the subject of religion: "What distinguishes the current generation of self-help literature is the author's use of frankly religious language. Words like 'soul,' 'sacred,' 'spiritual' and 'sacramental' turn up regularly in today's best-selling guidebooks."

Bookstore shelves are lined with authors from all sorts of religious persuasions. New Age mixes with Christian and Buddhist literature. Even psychology now adds the perspective of religion and spirituality to self-help books.

Such an array can be confusing enough. Add to that the "sacred" books of the world's major religions—the Bible, the Koran, the Book of Mormon, the sayings of Buddha, and many others—and people's search for meaning can take many paths.

One of these "sacred" books differs from all the others. It makes unique claims, and it points to a God who is different from those of any other religion.

What book is that? What makes it different? The passages that follow identify that sacred book as the Bible. Learn what the Bible has to say about itself.

What the Bible Tells Us

Above all, you must understand that no prophecy of Scripture came about by the prophet's own interpretation. For prophecy never had its origin in the will of man, but men spoke from God as they were carried along by the Holy Spirit. (2 Peter 1:20-21)

All Scripture is God-breathed and is useful for teaching, rebuking, correcting and training in righteousness, so that the man of God may be thoroughly equipped for every good work. (2 Timothy 3:16-17)

How the Bible Relates

1. Where did the prophecies, or messages, of Scripture come from?

2. What picture comes to mind when it says Scripture is "God-breathed"? What do you think this means?

3. For what is Scripture useful?

4. What does it equip people to do?

5. Why might it be worthwhile to read the Bible?

The Bottom Line

The Bible claims that it was written by the inspiration of God the Holy Spirit. This alone makes it different from any other book in the world—and worth studying. Since its power can change lives, correct faults, and equip people for doing good, we need to seriously consider this book.

Prayer

Dear God, help me to read and understand this book, the Bible. If it is truly from you, show me your power by changing my life through what I read. Amen.

A Final Word

God's word is alive and working. It is sharper than a sword sharpened on both sides. It cuts all the way into us, where the soul and the spirit are joined. It cuts to the center of our joints and our bones. And God's word judges the thoughts and feelings in our hearts. Nothing in all the world can be hidden from God. Everything is clear and lies open before him. *(The writer of Hebrews in Hebrews 4:12, New Century Version)*

2: The Truth About the Bible

Beginnings

What kinds of books—both religious and nonreligious—determine how people live? What religious books—old or new—do people read and use today? Have you ever read any of them, including the Bible? Do you think that the Bible is different from any of these books? Why or why not?

What's Happening Today

In November 1994, *Newsweek* came out with a powerful cover story: "In Search of the Sacred." Recent polls of North American society show that "millions of Americans are embarking on a search for the sacred in their lives. . . . The seekers fit no particular profile. They include Wall Street investment bankers who spend their lunch hours in Bible study groups, artists rediscovering religious themes, fitness addicts who have traded aerobics classes for meditation and other spiritual exercises. No matter what path they take, the seekers are united by a sincere desire to find answers to proud questions, to understand their place in the cosmos."

Newsweek notes the number of books appearing on the subject of religion: "What distinguishes the current generation of self-help literature is the author's use of frankly religious language. Words like 'soul,' 'sacred,' 'spiritual' and 'sacramental' turn up regularly in today's best-selling guidebooks."

Bookstore shelves are lined with authors from all sorts of religious persuasions. New Age mixes with Christian and Buddhist literature. Even psychology now adds the perspective of religion and spirituality to self-help books.

Such an array can be confusing enough. Add to that the "sacred" books of the world's major religions—the Bible, the Koran, the Book of Mormon, the sayings of Buddha, and many others—and people's search for meaning can take many paths.

One of these "sacred" books differs from all the others. It makes unique claims, and it points to a God who is different from those of any other religion.

What book is that? What makes it different? The passages that follow identify that sacred book as the Bible. Learn what the Bible has to say about itself.

What the Bible Tells Us

Above all, you must understand that no prophecy of Scripture came about by the prophet's own interpretation. For prophecy never had its origin in the will of man, but men spoke from God as they were carried along by the Holy Spirit. (2 Peter 1:20-21)

All Scripture is God-breathed and is useful for teaching, rebuking, correcting and training in righteousness, so that the man of God may be thoroughly equipped for every good work. (2 Timothy 3:16-17)

How the Bible Relates

1. Where did the prophecies, or messages, of Scripture come from?

2. What picture comes to mind when it says Scripture is "God-breathed"? What do you think this means?

3. For what is Scripture useful?

4. What does it equip people to do?

5. Why might it be worthwhile to read the Bible?

The Bottom Line

The Bible claims that it was written by the inspiration of God the Holy Spirit. This alone makes it different from any other book in the world—and worth studying. Since its power can change lives, correct faults, and equip people for doing good, we need to seriously consider this book.

Prayer

Dear God, help me to read and understand this book, the Bible. If it is truly from you, show me your power by changing my life through what I read. Amen.

A Final Word

God's word is alive and working. It is sharper than a sword sharpened on both sides. It cuts all the way into us, where the soul and the spirit are joined. It cuts to the center of our joints and our bones. And God's word judges the thoughts and feelings in our hearts. Nothing in all the world can be hidden from God. Everything is clear and lies open before him. *(The writer of Hebrews in Hebrews 4:12, New Century Version)*

2: The Truth About the Bible

Beginnings

What kinds of books—both religious and nonreligious—determine how people live? What religious books—old or new—do people read and use today? Have you ever read any of them, including the Bible? Do you think that the Bible is different from any of these books? Why or why not?

What's Happening Today

In November 1994, *Newsweek* came out with a powerful cover story: "In Search of the Sacred." Recent polls of North American society show that "millions of Americans are embarking on a search for the sacred in their lives. . . . The seekers fit no particular profile. They include Wall Street investment bankers who spend their lunch hours in Bible study groups, artists rediscovering religious themes, fitness addicts who have traded aerobics classes for meditation and other spiritual exercises. No matter what path they take, the seekers are united by a sincere desire to find answers to proud questions, to understand their place in the cosmos."

Newsweek notes the number of books appearing on the subject of religion: "What distinguishes the current generation of self-help literature is the author's use of frankly religious language. Words like 'soul,' 'sacred,' 'spiritual' and 'sacramental' turn up regularly in today's best-selling guidebooks."

Bookstore shelves are lined with authors from all sorts of religious persuasions. New Age mixes with Christian and Buddhist literature. Even psychology now adds the perspective of religion and spirituality to self-help books.

Such an array can be confusing enough. Add to that the "sacred" books of the world's major religions—the Bible, the Koran, the Book of Mormon, the sayings of Buddha, and many others—and people's search for meaning can take many paths.

One of these "sacred" books differs from all the others. It makes unique claims, and it points to a God who is different from those of any other religion.

What book is that? What makes it different? The passages that follow identify that sacred book as the Bible. Learn what the Bible has to say about itself.

What the Bible Tells Us

Above all, you must understand that no prophecy of Scripture came about by the prophet's own interpretation. For prophecy never had its origin in the will of man, but men spoke from God as they were carried along by the Holy Spirit. (2 Peter 1:20-21)

All Scripture is God-breathed and is useful for teaching, rebuking, correcting and training in righteousness, so that the man of God may be thoroughly equipped for every good work. (2 Timothy 3:16-17)

How the Bible Relates

1. Where did the prophecies, or messages, of Scripture come from?

2. What picture comes to mind when it says Scripture is "God-breathed"? What do you think this means?

3. For what is Scripture useful?

4. What does it equip people to do?

5. Why might it be worthwhile to read the Bible?

The Bottom Line

The Bible claims that it was written by the inspiration of God the Holy Spirit. This alone makes it different from any other book in the world—and worth studying. Since its power can change lives, correct faults, and equip people for doing good, we need to seriously consider this book.

Prayer

Dear God, help me to read and understand this book, the Bible. If it is truly from you, show me your power by changing my life through what I read. Amen.

A Final Word

God's word is alive and working. It is sharper than a sword sharpened on both sides. It cuts all the way into us, where the soul and the spirit are joined. It cuts to the center of our joints and our bones. And God's word judges the thoughts and feelings in our hearts. Nothing in all the world can be hidden from God. Everything is clear and lies open before him. *(The writer of Hebrews in Hebrews 4:12, New Century Version)*

The Whole Truth and Nothing But the Truth

3: The Truth About Truth

Introductory Notes

The concept of truth can be approached from many different angles. Some people like to maintain a philosophical level as they ask Pilate's question, "What is truth?" Your group members' approach will probably be less philosophical and more practical. They will be more interested in how they can believe what they are being told is true. As their leader, you will have to earn their trust as one who tells the truth.

This does not mean that you must know all the answers. For many in your group, hearing Christ's claims, possibly for the first time, will be enough. Always be sensitive in your responses and never be defensive. Remember that your group members are free to believe what they want. They will likely cling to what they believe is true. Your job is simply to present the claims of Christ. The Holy Spirit will enlighten them. Winning arguments is not your top priority. Gently revealing the truth is!

Beginning the Session

Greet your group members warmly and follow up on previous conversations and concerns. Encourage group members to get to know each other by asking nonthreatening questions that will open them up a bit. When everyone has had a chance to "connect," distribute the discussion handouts and start with the "Beginnings" questions.

 In the extended format, you may wish to briefly recap your discussion of the past two sessions. Ask if anyone has further insights, questions, or experiences that relate to those two sessions. A member may have experienced a dramatic answer to prayer or may wish to share a new insight. Share those now, before you get into a new topic of discussion.

Beginnings

When did you first discover that something you firmly believed in was actually false? For example, when did you find out that Santa Claus or Superman was only imaginary? How did you feel then? If possible, share a time when someone deceived you to the point that it had a major impact on your life.

Read these questions aloud to your group (unless some in your group have expressed a willingness to read aloud). You may hear some humorous stories here, as well as painful accounts of lies and betrayal. Don't do any "teaching" at this point; simply listen and note the per-

spectives from which your group members approach the subject of truth.

What's Happening Today

Reading through this section aloud should help group members discover how the question "What is truth?" connects with their daily lives. They may recall more experiences to share, or maybe a recent case in the news would illustrate these points. If time allows, give opportunity for sharing; otherwise move to the Scripture readings.

What the Bible Tells Us

Now that your group has met a few times, perhaps you have willing volunteers to read. You may want to ask three different people to read the three sections of the Scripture passage.

Introduce the reading by telling your group that the three passages all come from John's gospel in the New Testament. John was one of Jesus' closest friends. He was also one of the twelve disciples whom Jesus chose especially to teach his ways. John's purpose in writing his gospel was to show that Jesus Christ was indeed the truth—the only way to God.

How the Bible Relates

1. How does Jesus assure us that he is telling the truth? What claims does he make about himself in John 7:16-18?

In John 7, Jesus establishes his credibility as a reliable teacher. But he doesn't just try to prove his own authority. **How does he also ask his listeners to examine themselves? What must they do before they can know for certain that Jesus' teachings are trustworthy? Why do you think he was concerned about his listeners?** As one commentator put it, "His hearers had raised the question of his competence as a teacher. He raises the question of their competence as hearers."

Teachers in Jesus' day often based their teachings and authority on that of past teachers. Jesus claims to have received his teachings and authority from God. He challenged his listeners to observe him and then determine whether they should listen to his message. Your group members may know very little about Jesus' life, whereas those who were listening to Jesus had seen and heard many amazing things about him. You may be able to determine what your group members know by asking this question: **What about Jesus' life might lead you to** trust him—or at least make you want to trust him? How might even his prominence in history compel us to take a closer look at him? Even our calendars are ordered by the historical fact of his birth—either before or after his birth. Surely that commands further examination.

Many people today find Jesus a very compelling personality. It makes sense to trust him when he talks about the truth. At this point (or when you discuss the other passages of this session) some of your members might ask whether Jesus actually said the things he is quoted as saying. If so, listen to their concerns, but tell them that reliable Bible scholars side with the gospel accounts. F. F. Bruce points out that the writings of the New Testament present us with the most reliable and historically accurate accounts of Jesus' life in the world. If any group members are interested in pursuing this further, you might refer them to chapter 7 of *Why Should Anyone Believe Anything at All?* by James Sire, or *The New Testament Documents: Are They Reliable?* by F. F. Bruce.

How do contemporary media depict Jesus Christ? Based on this Scripture passage, how accurately do you think Jesus is portrayed? Is he portrayed as trustworthy and reliable? Explain. Ask group members to think of examples from recent movies, television, plays, or books that present a view of Jesus or Christianity. **What is our responsibility in responding to the stereotypes of Christianity?** Anyone can write an opinion on a subject, especially regarding the claims of Christ, but one must carefully examine the author's credentials and weigh the evidence before deciding to believe. For this first question, emphasize that we can believe what Jesus says about truth because he is a reliable source.

 In the expanded format, discuss the relationship between doing God's will and understanding his truth. **What does it mean "to do God's will"? Do you know anyone who does God's will? How would you describe his or her lifestyle?** Experiencing something will confirm or deny its correctness, importance, or truthfulness. Jesus challenges his readers to seek God so they may have a clearer picture of the truth.

2. No leader of any major religious group has ever made the claims Jesus made in John 14:6. What do you think Jesus is saying about himself?

When Jesus lays claim to being the truth, he is not speaking philosophically. Rather, he is saying that he embodies the truth about God. Commentator William Barclay writes, "Many men have told us the truth, but no man ever embodied it." **What is the difference between saying, "I *am* the truth" and "I *speak* the truth"?** Speculating on the essence of truth may be mentally challenging, but Jesus deals with this on a deeper level when he says, "I am the truth." He cloaks philosophical arguments with flesh and blood.

This, after all, is supremely important. People looking for truth and reality need only look to the historical figure

Jesus, of whom his friend John wrote. (John's evangelistic purpose in writing his gospel is "that you may believe that Jesus is the Christ . . . and that by believing you may have life in his name [20:31].) If we want to know what God is like and what he wants from us, we need only look to Jesus for the answer. If we want to know how to live, he is our example. If we want to know about what happens after death, we need only study Jesus' teachings on the subject.

 In the extended format, discuss what it means to "come to the Father." You might want to introduce the idea that Jesus has provided the way for people to have a saving relationship to God. Be sensitive to where your group members are at this point. You can keep it simple (Jesus introduces us to God), or you can explain the essence of the gospel: Jesus' death makes it possible for us to be accepted and loved by a holy and righteous God, just as we are.

3. Why did Jesus come into the world?

Take a few minutes to briefly summarize the context of John 18:36-38a. (Review beforehand Matthew 26-27.) **What were the charges against Jesus? Why did people think that he had come? Why might that have been a threat to the Roman government?** Help your group to see that Pilate's concern was merely political.

What was the real reason for Jesus' coming? How might that have confused Pilate? Apparently, Pilate and Jesus are speaking past each other. Pilate tries to pin down a political motive for Jesus' actions. Jesus speaks of a ministry from God that far transcends any political boundaries or ambitions. He came simply that people might know the truth. **What "truth" do you think God wants to communicate to us through Jesus?** Use this question as an opportunity to discover how much your group members have grasped of Jesus' ministry—and as a possible opening to explain simply and clearly the truth of our broken relationship with God and God's loving design to heal that relationship.

4. Who listens to Jesus?

This question, though it sounds innocent enough, will gently prod your group members to look at themselves. Are they on the side of truth? Asking the following questions may be helpful. **What makes it difficult for us to accept the truth about ourselves? When is it hard to face the truth? What are the risks of rejecting a true diagnosis? What do you think is ultimately the better choice—honestly seeking the truth regardless of the consequences or choosing to believe comfortable lies?**

Jesus says that people who truly desire to hear the truth will listen to him. Tell your group that with his question, Pilate abruptly cut off his interview of Jesus, apparently uninterested in Jesus' response to his question. Pilate desired to keep the discussion on an intellectual plane rather than bringing it down to a life-changing level. **Why might it have been threatening for Pilate, the Roman governor, to do so? How great was the risk?**

5. Can you identify with Pilate's final question to Jesus? What would you have asked Jesus?

Use this last question to learn where your group members are in their quest for truth. Are their questions more philosophical than personal? Listen carefully to what they would ask Jesus. Perhaps some of their questions will come up in later sessions. Pray that the Holy Spirit will work in their lives and induce genuine searching. Pray that, unlike Pilate, they will seek answers to their questions and act on the answers they receive.

The Bottom Line

Jesus not only points us to the truth, but he also embodies truth. If we wish to learn more about truth, we must learn more about Jesus.

Read this statement as a summary and review of the basic truths of the Scripture you have read. Assure your group that they will learn more about Jesus in coming sessions and that another session focuses on Jesus' life and teachings. Pray that they will be interested enough to pursue that study as well.

Optional Prayer Time

If the following prayer applies to the needs of your group, use it as part of your closing prayer time. Again, follow up on prayer needs and practical ways to "build bridges" in your group before you close in prayer. Ask God to send his Holy Spirit to each person during the coming week in order to give them greater understanding into the question "What is truth?" and Jesus' claim to be the truth.

Prayer

Dear God, in a world that promises so much but delivers so little, help us to find what is true and reliable. Amen.

A Final Word

I want you to know fully God's secret truth. That truth is Christ himself. And in him all the treasures of wisdom and knowledge are safely kept. (*The apostle Paul in Colossians 2:2-3, New Century Version*)

3: The Truth About Truth

Introductory Notes

The concept of truth can be approached from many different angles. Some people like to maintain a philosophical level as they ask Pilate's question, "What is truth?" Your group members' approach will probably be less philosophical and more practical. They will be more interested in how they can believe what they are being told is true. As their leader, you will have to earn their trust as one who tells the truth.

This does not mean that you must know all the answers. For many in your group, hearing Christ's claims, possibly for the first time, will be enough. Always be sensitive in your responses and never be defensive. Remember that your group members are free to believe what they want. They will likely cling to what they believe is true. Your job is simply to present the claims of Christ. The Holy Spirit will enlighten them. Winning arguments is not your top priority. Gently revealing the truth is!

Beginning the Session

Greet your group members warmly and follow up on previous conversations and concerns. Encourage group members to get to know each other by asking nonthreatening questions that will open them up a bit. When everyone has had a chance to "connect," distribute the discussion handouts and start with the "Beginnings" questions.

 In the extended format, you may wish to briefly recap your discussion of the past two sessions. Ask if anyone has further insights, questions, or experiences that relate to those two sessions. A member may have experienced a dramatic answer to prayer or may wish to share a new insight. Share those now, before you get into a new topic of discussion.

Beginnings

When did you first discover that something you firmly believed in was actually false? For example, when did you find out that Santa Claus or Superman was only imaginary? How did you feel then? If possible, share a time when someone deceived you to the point that it had a major impact on your life.

Read these questions aloud to your group (unless some in your group have expressed a willingness to read aloud). You may hear some humorous stories here, as well as painful accounts of lies and betrayal. Don't do any "teaching" at this point; simply listen and note the per-spectives from which your group members approach the subject of truth.

What's Happening Today

Reading through this section aloud should help group members discover how the question "What is truth?" connects with their daily lives. They may recall more experiences to share, or maybe a recent case in the news would illustrate these points. If time allows, give opportunity for sharing; otherwise move to the Scripture readings.

What the Bible Tells Us

Now that your group has met a few times, perhaps you have willing volunteers to read. You may want to ask three different people to read the three sections of the Scripture passage.

Introduce the reading by telling your group that the three passages all come from John's gospel in the New Testament. John was one of Jesus' closest friends. He was also one of the twelve disciples whom Jesus chose especially to teach his ways. John's purpose in writing his gospel was to show that Jesus Christ was indeed the truth—the only way to God.

How the Bible Relates

1. How does Jesus assure us that he is telling the truth? What claims does he make about himself in John 7:16-18?

In John 7, Jesus establishes his credibility as a reliable teacher. But he doesn't just try to prove his own authority. **How does he also ask his listeners to examine themselves? What must they do before they can know for certain that Jesus' teachings are trustworthy? Why do you think he was concerned about his listeners?** As one commentator put it, "His hearers had raised the question of his competence as a teacher. He raises the question of their competence as hearers."

Teachers in Jesus' day often based their teachings and authority on that of past teachers. Jesus claims to have received his teachings and authority from God. He challenged his listeners to observe him and then determine whether they should listen to his message. Your group members may know very little about Jesus' life, whereas those who were listening to Jesus had seen and heard many amazing things about him. You may be able to determine what your group members know by asking this question: **What about Jesus' life might lead you to** trust him—or at least make you want to trust him? How might even his prominence in history compel us to take a closer look at him? Even our calendars are ordered by the historical fact of his birth—either before or after his birth. Surely that commands further examination.

Many people today find Jesus a very compelling personality. It makes sense to trust him when he talks about the truth. At this point (or when you discuss the other passages of this session) some of your members might ask whether Jesus actually said the things he is quoted as saying. If so, listen to their concerns, but tell them that reliable Bible scholars side with the gospel accounts. F. F. Bruce points out that the writings of the New Testament present us with the most reliable and historically accurate accounts of Jesus' life in the world. If any group members are interested in pursuing this further, you might refer them to chapter 7 of *Why Should Anyone Believe Anything at All?* by James Sire, or *The New Testament Documents: Are They Reliable?* by F. F. Bruce.

How do contemporary media depict Jesus Christ? Based on this Scripture passage, how accurately do you think Jesus is portrayed? Is he portrayed as trustworthy and reliable? Explain. Ask group members to think of examples from recent movies, television, plays, or books that present a view of Jesus or Christianity. **What is our responsibility in responding to the stereotypes of Christianity?** Anyone can write an opinion on a subject, especially regarding the claims of Christ, but one must carefully examine the author's credentials and weigh the evidence before deciding to believe. For this first question, emphasize that we can believe what Jesus says about truth because he is a reliable source.

 In the expanded format, discuss the relationship between doing God's will and understanding his truth. **What does it mean "to do God's will"? Do you know anyone who does God's will? How would you describe his or her lifestyle?** Experiencing something will confirm or deny its correctness, importance, or truthfulness. Jesus challenges his readers to seek God so they may have a clearer picture of the truth.

2. No leader of any major religious group has ever made the claims Jesus made in John 14:6. What do you think Jesus is saying about himself?

When Jesus lays claim to being the truth, he is not speaking philosophically. Rather, he is saying that he embodies the truth about God. Commentator William Barclay writes, "Many men have told us the truth, but no man ever embodied it." **What is the difference between saying, "I *am* the truth" and "I *speak* the truth"?** Speculating on the essence of truth may be mentally challenging, but Jesus deals with this on a deeper level when he says, "I am the truth." He cloaks philosophical arguments with flesh and blood.

This, after all, is supremely important. People looking for truth and reality need only look to the historical figure

Jesus, of whom his friend John wrote. (John's evangelistic purpose in writing his gospel is "that you may believe that Jesus is the Christ . . . and that by believing you may have life in his name [20:31].) If we want to know what God is like and what he wants from us, we need only look to Jesus for the answer. If we want to know how to live, he is our example. If we want to know about what happens after death, we need only study Jesus' teachings on the subject.

 In the extended format, discuss what it means to "come to the Father." You might want to introduce the idea that Jesus has provided the way for people to have a saving relationship to God. Be sensitive to where your group members are at this point. You can keep it simple (Jesus introduces us to God), or you can explain the essence of the gospel: Jesus' death makes it possible for us to be accepted and loved by a holy and righteous God, just as we are.

3. Why did Jesus come into the world?

Take a few minutes to briefly summarize the context of John 18:36-38a. (Review beforehand Matthew 26-27.) **What were the charges against Jesus? Why did people think that he had come? Why might that have been a threat to the Roman government?** Help your group to see that Pilate's concern was merely political.

What was the real reason for Jesus' coming? How might that have confused Pilate? Apparently, Pilate and Jesus are speaking past each other. Pilate tries to pin down a political motive for Jesus' actions. Jesus speaks of a ministry from God that far transcends any political boundaries or ambitions. He came simply that people might know the truth. **What "truth" do you think God wants to communicate to us through Jesus?** Use this question as an opportunity to discover how much your group members have grasped of Jesus' ministry—and as a possible opening to explain simply and clearly the truth of our broken relationship with God and God's loving design to heal that relationship.

4. Who listens to Jesus?

This question, though it sounds innocent enough, will gently prod your group members to look at themselves. Are they on the side of truth? Asking the following questions may be helpful. **What makes it difficult for us to accept the truth about ourselves? When is it hard to face the truth? What are the risks of rejecting a true diagnosis? What do you think is ultimately the better choice—honestly seeking the truth regardless of the consequences or choosing to believe comfortable lies?**

Jesus says that people who truly desire to hear the truth will listen to him. Tell your group that with his question, Pilate abruptly cut off his interview of Jesus, apparently uninterested in Jesus' response to his question. Pilate desired to keep the discussion on an intellectual plane rather than bringing it down to a life-changing level. **Why might it have been threatening for Pilate, the Roman governor, to do so? How great was the risk?**

5. Can you identify with Pilate's final question to Jesus? What would you have asked Jesus?

Use this last question to learn where your group members are in their quest for truth. Are their questions more philosophical than personal? Listen carefully to what they would ask Jesus. Perhaps some of their questions will come up in later sessions. Pray that the Holy Spirit will work in their lives and induce genuine searching. Pray that, unlike Pilate, they will seek answers to their questions and act on the answers they receive.

The Bottom Line

Jesus not only points us to the truth, but he also embodies truth. If we wish to learn more about truth, we must learn more about Jesus.

Read this statement as a summary and review of the basic truths of the Scripture you have read. Assure your group that they will learn more about Jesus in coming sessions and that another session focuses on Jesus' life and teachings. Pray that they will be interested enough to pursue that study as well.

Optional Prayer Time

If the following prayer applies to the needs of your group, use it as part of your closing prayer time. Again, follow up on prayer needs and practical ways to "build bridges" in your group before you close in prayer. Ask God to send his Holy Spirit to each person during the coming week in order to give them greater understanding into the question "What is truth?" and Jesus' claim to be the truth.

Prayer

Dear God, in a world that promises so much but delivers so little, help us to find what is true and reliable. Amen.

A Final Word

I want you to know fully God's secret truth. That truth is Christ himself. And in him all the treasures of wisdom and knowledge are safely kept. *(The apostle Paul in Colossians 2:2-3, New Century Version)*

3: The Truth About Truth

Beginnings

When did you first discover that something you firmly believed in was actually false? For example, when did you find out that Santa Claus or Superman was only imaginary? How did you feel then? If possible, share a time when someone deceived you to the point that it had a major impact on your life.

What's Happening Today

We live in a time of universal distrust. We often find ourselves thinking that certain people are not telling us the truth. This includes not only used car salesmen but also politicians. A recent lead article in *Time* magazine states, "The public now assumes lying on the part of its representatives because it expects them to lie. . . . Politicians know that they are widely perceived as liars. It is no wonder that we listen to campaign promises with a 'grain of salt.'"

Other events feed our distrust. A young mother gains our overwhelming sympathy when she tells us that her young sons have been kidnapped, and then she admits drowning them strapped securely in the family car. Well-known celebrities deny committing heinous crimes but courts of law subsequently find them guilty.

Some religious leaders gain followers by convincing them to believe all that they say. Unfortunately, the truth surfaces too late and the world is riveted to news photos from places like Jonestown, Guyana, and Waco.

Who is telling the truth anymore? What can we believe? Is the tumor benign or malignant? Has the mechanic really fixed our car's brakes? Is our teenage son at the party as he said he would be?

In every area of life, we want to know the straight scoop; we don't want to waste our time with false promises. We want people to tell it like it is.

To know the truth in the realm of faith is vitally important. All religions lay claim to the truth, but which one should we believe? Which one is true? Sincerity of belief is not the issue. Many sincere people in the world believe lies. We are interested in reality and reliability.

When Jesus lived on earth, he made some astonishing statements and amazing claims. He often spoke of truth. In fact, he began most of his teachings by saying, "I tell you the truth. . . ." Perhaps the most remarkable claim Jesus made is the statement: "I am the truth." The following Scripture from the gospel of John, a recorded history of Jesus' life, gives important information on how to find truth.

What the Bible Tells Us

Jesus answered, "My teaching is not my own. It comes from him who sent me. If anyone chooses to do God's will, he will find out whether my teaching comes from God or whether I speak on my own. He who speaks on his own does so to gain honor for himself, but he who works for the honor of the one who sent him is a man of truth; there is nothing false about him." (John 7:16-18)

Jesus answered, "I am the way, the truth and the life. No one comes to the Father except through me." (John 14:6)

Note: As a human, Jesus lived during the time of the Roman empire. At the end of his ministry, he was accused of political treason by his countrymen. The following conversation took place as Jesus stood before the Roman governor, Pilate, during his trial.

Jesus said, "My kingdom is not of this world. If it were, my servants would fight to prevent my arrest by the Jews. But now my kingdom is from another place." "You are a king, then!" said Pilate. Jesus answered, "You are right in saying I am a king. In fact, for this reason I was born, and for this I came into the world, to testify to the truth. Everyone on the side of truth listens to me." "What is truth?" Pilate asked. (John 18:36-38a)

How the Bible Relates

1. How does Jesus assure us that he is telling the truth? What claims does he make about himself in John 7:16-18?

2. No leader of any major religious group has ever made the claims Jesus made in John 14:6. What do you think Jesus is saying about himself?

3. Why did Jesus come into the world?

4. Who listens to Jesus?

5. Can you identify with Pilate's final question to Jesus? What would you have asked Jesus?

The Bottom Line

Jesus not only points us to the truth, but he also embodies truth. If we wish to learn more about truth, we must learn more about Jesus.

Prayer

Dear God, in a world that promises so much but delivers so little, help us to find what is true and reliable. Amen.

A Final Word

I want you to know fully God's secret truth. That truth is Christ himself. And in him all the treasures of wisdom and knowledge are safely kept. *(The apostle Paul in Colossians 2:2-3, New Century Version)*

3: The Truth About Truth

Beginnings

When did you first discover that something you firmly believed in was actually false? For example, when did you find out that Santa Claus or Superman was only imaginary? How did you feel then? If possible, share a time when someone deceived you to the point that it had a major impact on your life.

What's Happening Today

We live in a time of universal distrust. We often find ourselves thinking that certain people are not telling us the truth. This includes not only used car salesmen but also politicians. A recent lead article in *Time* magazine states, "The public now assumes lying on the part of its representatives because it expects them to lie. . . . Politicians know that they are widely perceived as liars. It is no wonder that we listen to campaign promises with a 'grain of salt.'"

Other events feed our distrust. A young mother gains our overwhelming sympathy when she tells us that her young sons have been kidnapped, and then she admits drowning them strapped securely in the family car. Well-known celebrities deny committing heinous crimes but courts of law subsequently find them guilty.

Some religious leaders gain followers by convincing them to believe all that they say. Unfortunately, the truth surfaces too late and the world is riveted to news photos from places like Jonestown, Guyana, and Waco.

Who is telling the truth anymore? What can we believe? Is the tumor benign or malignant? Has the mechanic really fixed our car's brakes? Is our teenage son at the party as he said he would be?

In every area of life, we want to know the straight scoop; we don't want to waste our time with false promises. We want people to tell it like it is.

To know the truth in the realm of faith is vitally important. All religions lay claim to the truth, but which one should we believe? Which one is true? Sincerity of belief is not the issue. Many sincere people in the world believe lies. We are interested in reality and reliability.

When Jesus lived on earth, he made some astonishing statements and amazing claims. He often spoke of truth. In fact, he began most of his teachings by saying, "I tell you the truth. . . ." Perhaps the most remarkable claim Jesus made is the statement: "I am the truth." The following Scripture from the gospel of John, a recorded history of Jesus' life, gives important information on how to find truth.

What the Bible Tells Us

Jesus answered, "My teaching is not my own. It comes from him who sent me. If anyone chooses to do God's will, he will find out whether my teaching comes from God or whether I speak on my own. He who speaks on his own does so to gain honor for himself, but he who works for the honor of the one who sent him is a man of truth; there is nothing false about him." (John 7:16-18)

Jesus answered, "I am the way, the truth and the life. No one comes to the Father except through me." (John 14:6)

Note: As a human, Jesus lived during the time of the Roman empire. At the end of his ministry, he was accused of political treason by his countrymen. The following conversation took place as Jesus stood before the Roman governor, Pilate, during his trial.

Jesus said, "My kingdom is not of this world. If it were, my servants would fight to prevent my arrest by the Jews. But now my kingdom is from another place." "You are a king, then!" said Pilate. Jesus answered, "You are right in saying I am a king. In fact, for this reason I was born, and for this I came into the world, to testify to the truth. Everyone on the side of truth listens to me." "What is truth?" Pilate asked. (John 18:36-38a)

How the Bible Relates

1. How does Jesus assure us that he is telling the truth? What claims does he make about himself in John 7:16-18?

2. No leader of any major religious group has ever made the claims Jesus made in John 14:6. What do you think Jesus is saying about himself?

3. Why did Jesus come into the world?

4. Who listens to Jesus?

5. Can you identify with Pilate's final question to Jesus? What would you have asked Jesus?

The Bottom Line

Jesus not only points us to the truth, but he also embodies truth. If we wish to learn more about truth, we must learn more about Jesus.

Prayer

Dear God, in a world that promises so much but delivers so little, help us to find what is true and reliable. Amen.

A Final Word

I want you to know fully God's secret truth. That truth is Christ himself. And in him all the treasures of wisdom and knowledge are safely kept. *(The apostle Paul in Colossians 2:2-3, New Century Version)*

3: The Truth About Truth

Beginnings

When did you first discover that something you firmly believed in was actually false? For example, when did you find out that Santa Claus or Superman was only imaginary? How did you feel then? If possible, share a time when someone deceived you to the point that it had a major impact on your life.

What's Happening Today

We live in a time of universal distrust. We often find ourselves thinking that certain people are not telling us the truth. This includes not only used car salesmen but also politicians. A recent lead article in *Time* magazine states, "The public now assumes lying on the part of its representatives because it expects them to lie. . . . Politicians know that they are widely perceived as liars. It is no wonder that we listen to campaign promises with a 'grain of salt.'"

Other events feed our distrust. A young mother gains our overwhelming sympathy when she tells us that her young sons have been kidnapped, and then she admits drowning them strapped securely in the family car. Well-known celebrities deny committing heinous crimes but courts of law subsequently find them guilty.

Some religious leaders gain followers by convincing them to believe all that they say. Unfortunately, the truth surfaces too late and the world is riveted to news photos from places like Jonestown, Guyana, and Waco.

Who is telling the truth anymore? What can we believe? Is the tumor benign or malignant? Has the mechanic really fixed our car's brakes? Is our teenage son at the party as he said he would be?

In every area of life, we want to know the straight scoop; we don't want to waste our time with false promises. We want people to tell it like it is.

To know the truth in the realm of faith is vitally important. All religions lay claim to the truth, but which one should we believe? Which one is true? Sincerity of belief is not the issue. Many sincere people in the world believe lies. We are interested in reality and reliability.

When Jesus lived on earth, he made some astonishing statements and amazing claims. He often spoke of truth. In fact, he began most of his teachings by saying, "I tell you the truth. . . ." Perhaps the most remarkable claim Jesus made is the statement: "I am the truth." The following Scripture from the gospel of John, a recorded history of Jesus' life, gives important information on how to find truth.

What the Bible Tells Us

Jesus answered, "My teaching is not my own. It comes from him who sent me. If anyone chooses to do God's will, he will find out whether my teaching comes from God or whether I speak on my own. He who speaks on his own does so to gain honor for himself, but he who works for the honor of the one who sent him is a man of truth; there is nothing false about him." (John 7:16-18)

Jesus answered, "I am the way, the truth and the life. No one comes to the Father except through me." (John 14:6)

Note: As a human, Jesus lived during the time of the Roman empire. At the end of his ministry, he was accused of political treason by his countrymen. The following conversation took place as Jesus stood before the Roman governor, Pilate, during his trial.

Jesus said, "My kingdom is not of this world. If it were, my servants would fight to prevent my arrest by the Jews. But now my kingdom is from another place." "You are a king, then!" said Pilate. Jesus answered, "You are right in saying I am a king. In fact, for this reason I was born, and for this I came into the world, to testify to the truth. Everyone on the side of truth listens to me." "What is truth?" Pilate asked. (John 18:36-38a)

How the Bible Relates

1. How does Jesus assure us that he is telling the truth? What claims does he make about himself in John 7:16-18?

2. No leader of any major religious group has ever made the claims Jesus made in John 14:6. What do you think Jesus is saying about himself?

3. Why did Jesus come into the world?

4. Who listens to Jesus?

5. Can you identify with Pilate's final question to Jesus? What would you have asked Jesus?

The Bottom Line

Jesus not only points us to the truth, but he also embodies truth. If we wish to learn more about truth, we must learn more about Jesus.

Prayer

Dear God, in a world that promises so much but delivers so little, help us to find what is true and reliable. Amen.

A Final Word

I want you to know fully God's secret truth. That truth is Christ himself. And in him all the treasures of wisdom and knowledge are safely kept. *(The apostle Paul in Colossians 2:2-3, New Century Version)*

3: The Truth About Truth

Beginnings

When did you first discover that something you firmly believed in was actually false? For example, when did you find out that Santa Claus or Superman was only imaginary? How did you feel then? If possible, share a time when someone deceived you to the point that it had a major impact on your life.

What's Happening Today

We live in a time of universal distrust. We often find ourselves thinking that certain people are not telling us the truth. This includes not only used car salesmen but also politicians. A recent lead article in *Time* magazine states, "The public now assumes lying on the part of its representatives because it expects them to lie. . . . Politicians know that they are widely perceived as liars. It is no wonder that we listen to campaign promises with a 'grain of salt.'"

Other events feed our distrust. A young mother gains our overwhelming sympathy when she tells us that her young sons have been kidnapped, and then she admits drowning them strapped securely in the family car. Well-known celebrities deny committing heinous crimes but courts of law subsequently find them guilty.

Some religious leaders gain followers by convincing them to believe all that they say. Unfortunately, the truth surfaces too late and the world is riveted to news photos from places like Jonestown, Guyana, and Waco.

Who is telling the truth anymore? What can we believe? Is the tumor benign or malignant? Has the mechanic really fixed our car's brakes? Is our teenage son at the party as he said he would be?

In every area of life, we want to know the straight scoop; we don't want to waste our time with false promises. We want people to tell it like it is.

To know the truth in the realm of faith is vitally important. All religions lay claim to the truth, but which one should we believe? Which one is true? Sincerity of belief is not the issue. Many sincere people in the world believe lies. We are interested in reality and reliability.

When Jesus lived on earth, he made some astonishing statements and amazing claims. He often spoke of truth. In fact, he began most of his teachings by saying, "I tell you the truth. . . ." Perhaps the most remarkable claim Jesus made is the statement: "I am the truth." The following Scripture from the gospel of John, a recorded history of Jesus' life, gives important information on how to find truth.

What the Bible Tells Us

Jesus answered, "My teaching is not my own. It comes from him who sent me. If anyone chooses to do God's will, he will find out whether my teaching comes from God or whether I speak on my own. He who speaks on his own does so to gain honor for himself, but he who works for the honor of the one who sent him is a man of truth; there is nothing false about him." (John 7:16-18)

Jesus answered, "I am the way, the truth and the life. No one comes to the Father except through me." (John 14:6)

Note: As a human, Jesus lived during the time of the Roman empire. At the end of his ministry, he was accused of political treason by his countrymen. The following conversation took place as Jesus stood before the Roman governor, Pilate, during his trial.

Jesus said, "My kingdom is not of this world. If it were, my servants would fight to prevent my arrest by the Jews. But now my kingdom is from another place." "You are a king, then!" said Pilate. Jesus answered, "You are right in saying I am a king. In fact, for this reason I was born, and for this I came into the world, to testify to the truth. Everyone on the side of truth listens to me." "What is truth?" Pilate asked. (John 18:36-38a)

How the Bible Relates

1. How does Jesus assure us that he is telling the truth? What claims does he make about himself in John 7:16-18?

2. No leader of any major religious group has ever made the claims Jesus made in John 14:6. What do you think Jesus is saying about himself?

3. Why did Jesus come into the world?

4. Who listens to Jesus?

5. Can you identify with Pilate's final question to Jesus? What would you have asked Jesus?

The Bottom Line

Jesus not only points us to the truth, but he also embodies truth. If we wish to learn more about truth, we must learn more about Jesus.

Prayer

Dear God, in a world that promises so much but delivers so little, help us to find what is true and reliable. Amen.

A Final Word

I want you to know fully God's secret truth. That truth is Christ himself. And in him all the treasures of wisdom and knowledge are safely kept. *(The apostle Paul in Colossians 2:2-3, New Century Version)*

3: The Truth About Truth

Beginnings

When did you first discover that something you firmly believed in was actually false? For example, when did you find out that Santa Claus or Superman was only imaginary? How did you feel then? If possible, share a time when someone deceived you to the point that it had a major impact on your life.

What's Happening Today

We live in a time of universal distrust. We often find ourselves thinking that certain people are not telling us the truth. This includes not only used car salesmen but also politicians. A recent lead article in *Time* magazine states, "The public now assumes lying on the part of its representatives because it expects them to lie.... Politicians know that they are widely perceived as liars. It is no wonder that we listen to campaign promises with a 'grain of salt.'"

Other events feed our distrust. A young mother gains our overwhelming sympathy when she tells us that her young sons have been kidnapped, and then she admits drowning them strapped securely in the family car. Well-known celebrities deny committing heinous crimes but courts of law subsequently find them guilty.

Some religious leaders gain followers by convincing them to believe all that they say. Unfortunately, the truth surfaces too late and the world is riveted to news photos from places like Jonestown, Guyana, and Waco.

Who is telling the truth anymore? What can we believe? Is the tumor benign or malignant? Has the mechanic really fixed our car's brakes? Is our teenage son at the party as he said he would be?

In every area of life, we want to know the straight scoop; we don't want to waste our time with false promises. We want people to tell it like it is.

To know the truth in the realm of faith is vitally important. All religions lay claim to the truth, but which one should we believe? Which one is true? Sincerity of belief is not the issue. Many sincere people in the world believe lies. We are interested in reality and reliability.

When Jesus lived on earth, he made some astonishing statements and amazing claims. He often spoke of truth. In fact, he began most of his teachings by saying, "I tell you the truth...." Perhaps the most remarkable claim Jesus made is the statement: "I am the truth." The following Scripture from the gospel of John, a recorded history of Jesus' life, gives important information on how to find truth.

What the Bible Tells Us

Jesus answered, "My teaching is not my own. It comes from him who sent me. If anyone chooses to do God's will, he will find out whether my teaching comes from God or whether I speak on my own. He who speaks on his own does so to gain honor for himself, but he who works for the honor of the one who sent him is a man of truth; there is nothing false about him." (John 7:16-18)

Jesus answered, "I am the way, the truth and the life. No one comes to the Father except through me." (John 14:6)

Note: As a human, Jesus lived during the time of the Roman empire. At the end of his ministry, he was accused of political treason by his countrymen. The following conversation took place as Jesus stood before the Roman governor, Pilate, during his trial.

Jesus said, "My kingdom is not of this world. If it were, my servants would fight to prevent my arrest by the Jews. But now my kingdom is from another place." "You are a king, then!" said Pilate. Jesus answered, "You are right in saying I am a king. In fact, for this reason I was born, and for this I came into the world, to testify to the truth. Everyone on the side of truth listens to me." "What is truth?" Pilate asked. (John 18:36-38a)

How the Bible Relates

1. How does Jesus assure us that he is telling the truth? What claims does he make about himself in John 7:16-18?

2. No leader of any major religious group has ever made the claims Jesus made in John 14:6. What do you think Jesus is saying about himself?

3. Why did Jesus come into the world?

4. Who listens to Jesus?

5. Can you identify with Pilate's final question to Jesus? What would you have asked Jesus?

The Bottom Line

Jesus not only points us to the truth, but he also embodies truth. If we wish to learn more about truth, we must learn more about Jesus.

Prayer

Dear God, in a world that promises so much but delivers so little, help us to find what is true and reliable. Amen.

A Final Word

I want you to know fully God's secret truth. That truth is Christ himself. And in him all the treasures of wisdom and knowledge are safely kept. *(The apostle Paul in Colossians 2:2-3, New Century Version)*

3: The Truth About Truth

Beginnings

When did you first discover that something you firmly believed in was actually false? For example, when did you find out that Santa Claus or Superman was only imaginary? How did you feel then? If possible, share a time when someone deceived you to the point that it had a major impact on your life.

What's Happening Today

We live in a time of universal distrust. We often find ourselves thinking that certain people are not telling us the truth. This includes not only used car salesmen but also politicians. A recent lead article in *Time* magazine states, "The public now assumes lying on the part of its representatives because it expects them to lie.... Politicians know that they are widely perceived as liars. It is no wonder that we listen to campaign promises with a 'grain of salt.'"

Other events feed our distrust. A young mother gains our overwhelming sympathy when she tells us that her young sons have been kidnapped, and then she admits drowning them strapped securely in the family car. Well-known celebrities deny committing heinous crimes but courts of law subsequently find them guilty.

Some religious leaders gain followers by convincing them to believe all that they say. Unfortunately, the truth surfaces too late and the world is riveted to news photos from places like Jonestown, Guyana, and Waco.

Who is telling the truth anymore? What can we believe? Is the tumor benign or malignant? Has the mechanic really fixed our car's brakes? Is our teenage son at the party as he said he would be?

In every area of life, we want to know the straight scoop; we don't want to waste our time with false promises. We want people to tell it like it is.

To know the truth in the realm of faith is vitally important. All religions lay claim to the truth, but which one should we believe? Which one is true? Sincerity of belief is not the issue. Many sincere people in the world believe lies. We are interested in reality and reliability.

When Jesus lived on earth, he made some astonishing statements and amazing claims. He often spoke of truth. In fact, he began most of his teachings by saying, "I tell you the truth. ..." Perhaps the most remarkable claim Jesus made is the statement: "I am the truth." The following Scripture from the gospel of John, a recorded history of Jesus' life, gives important information on how to find truth.

What the Bible Tells Us

Jesus answered, "My teaching is not my own. It comes from him who sent me. If anyone chooses to do God's will, he will find out whether my teaching comes from God or whether I speak on my own. He who speaks on his own does so to gain honor for himself, but he who works for the honor of the one who sent him is a man of truth; there is nothing false about him." (John 7:16-18)

Jesus answered, "I am the way, the truth and the life. No one comes to the Father except through me." (John 14:6)

Note: As a human, Jesus lived during the time of the Roman empire. At the end of his ministry, he was accused of political treason by his countrymen. The following conversation took place as Jesus stood before the Roman governor, Pilate, during his trial.

Jesus said, "My kingdom is not of this world. If it were, my servants would fight to prevent my arrest by the Jews. But now my kingdom is from another place." "You are a king, then!" said Pilate. Jesus answered, "You are right in saying I am a king. In fact, for this reason I was born, and for this I came into the world, to testify to the truth. Everyone on the side of truth listens to me." "What is truth?" Pilate asked. (John 18:36-38a)

How the Bible Relates

1. How does Jesus assure us that he is telling the truth? What claims does he make about himself in John 7:16-18?

2. No leader of any major religious group has ever made the claims Jesus made in John 14:6. What do you think Jesus is saying about himself?

3. Why did Jesus come into the world?

4. Who listens to Jesus?

5. Can you identify with Pilate's final question to Jesus? What would you have asked Jesus?

The Bottom Line

Jesus not only points us to the truth, but he also embodies truth. If we wish to learn more about truth, we must learn more about Jesus.

Prayer

Dear God, in a world that promises so much but delivers so little, help us to find what is true and reliable. Amen.

A Final Word

I want you to know fully God's secret truth. That truth is Christ himself. And in him all the treasures of wisdom and knowledge are safely kept. *(The apostle Paul in Colossians 2:2-3, New Century Version)*

3: The Truth About Truth

Beginnings

When did you first discover that something you firmly believed in was actually false? For example, when did you find out that Santa Claus or Superman was only imaginary? How did you feel then? If possible, share a time when someone deceived you to the point that it had a major impact on your life.

What's Happening Today

We live in a time of universal distrust. We often find ourselves thinking that certain people are not telling us the truth. This includes not only used car salesmen but also politicians. A recent lead article in *Time* magazine states, "The public now assumes lying on the part of its representatives because it expects them to lie. . . . Politicians know that they are widely perceived as liars. It is no wonder that we listen to campaign promises with a 'grain of salt.'"

Other events feed our distrust. A young mother gains our overwhelming sympathy when she tells us that her young sons have been kidnapped, and then she admits drowning them strapped securely in the family car. Well-known celebrities deny committing heinous crimes but courts of law subsequently find them guilty.

Some religious leaders gain followers by convincing them to believe all that they say. Unfortunately, the truth surfaces too late and the world is riveted to news photos from places like Jonestown, Guyana, and Waco.

Who is telling the truth anymore? What can we believe? Is the tumor benign or malignant? Has the mechanic really fixed our car's brakes? Is our teenage son at the party as he said he would be?

In every area of life, we want to know the straight scoop; we don't want to waste our time with false promises. We want people to tell it like it is.

To know the truth in the realm of faith is vitally important. All religions lay claim to the truth, but which one should we believe? Which one is true? Sincerity of belief is not the issue. Many sincere people in the world believe lies. We are interested in reality and reliability.

When Jesus lived on earth, he made some astonishing statements and amazing claims. He often spoke of truth. In fact, he began most of his teachings by saying, "I tell you the truth. . . ." Perhaps the most remarkable claim Jesus made is the statement: "I am the truth." The following Scripture from the gospel of John, a recorded history of Jesus' life, gives important information on how to find truth.

What the Bible Tells Us

Jesus answered, "My teaching is not my own. It comes from him who sent me. If anyone chooses to do God's will, he will find out whether my teaching comes from God or whether I speak on my own. He who speaks on his own does so to gain honor for himself, but he who works for the honor of the one who sent him is a man of truth; there is nothing false about him." (John 7:16-18)

Jesus answered, "I am the way, the truth and the life. No one comes to the Father except through me." (John 14:6)

Note: As a human, Jesus lived during the time of the Roman empire. At the end of his ministry, he was accused of political treason by his countrymen. The following conversation took place as Jesus stood before the Roman governor, Pilate, during his trial.

Jesus said, "My kingdom is not of this world. If it were, my servants would fight to prevent my arrest by the Jews. But now my kingdom is from another place." "You are a king, then!" said Pilate. Jesus answered, "You are right in saying I am a king. In fact, for this reason I was born, and for this I came into the world, to testify to the truth. Everyone on the side of truth listens to me." "What is truth?" Pilate asked. (John 18:36-38a)

How the Bible Relates

1. How does Jesus assure us that he is telling the truth? What claims does he make about himself in John 7:16-18?

2. No leader of any major religious group has ever made the claims Jesus made in John 14:6. What do you think Jesus is saying about himself?

3. Why did Jesus come into the world?

4. Who listens to Jesus?

5. Can you identify with Pilate's final question to Jesus? What would you have asked Jesus?

The Bottom Line

Jesus not only points us to the truth, but he also embodies truth. If we wish to learn more about truth, we must learn more about Jesus.

Prayer

Dear God, in a world that promises so much but delivers so little, help us to find what is true and reliable. Amen.

A Final Word

I want you to know fully God's secret truth. That truth is Christ himself. And in him all the treasures of wisdom and knowledge are safely kept. *(The apostle Paul in Colossians 2:2-3, New Century Version)*

3: The Truth About Truth

Beginnings

When did you first discover that something you firmly believed in was actually false? For example, when did you find out that Santa Claus or Superman was only imaginary? How did you feel then? If possible, share a time when someone deceived you to the point that it had a major impact on your life.

What's Happening Today

We live in a time of universal distrust. We often find ourselves thinking that certain people are not telling us the truth. This includes not only used car salesmen but also politicians. A recent lead article in *Time* magazine states, "The public now assumes lying on the part of its representatives because it expects them to lie. . . . Politicians know that they are widely perceived as liars. It is no wonder that we listen to campaign promises with a 'grain of salt.'"

Other events feed our distrust. A young mother gains our overwhelming sympathy when she tells us that her young sons have been kidnapped, and then she admits drowning them strapped securely in the family car. Well-known celebrities deny committing heinous crimes but courts of law subsequently find them guilty.

Some religious leaders gain followers by convincing them to believe all that they say. Unfortunately, the truth surfaces too late and the world is riveted to news photos from places like Jonestown, Guyana, and Waco.

Who is telling the truth anymore? What can we believe? Is the tumor benign or malignant? Has the mechanic really fixed our car's brakes? Is our teenage son at the party as he said he would be?

In every area of life, we want to know the straight scoop; we don't want to waste our time with false promises. We want people to tell it like it is.

To know the truth in the realm of faith is vitally important. All religions lay claim to the truth, but which one should we believe? Which one is true? Sincerity of belief is not the issue. Many sincere people in the world believe lies. We are interested in reality and reliability.

When Jesus lived on earth, he made some astonishing statements and amazing claims. He often spoke of truth. In fact, he began most of his teachings by saying, "I tell you the truth. . . ." Perhaps the most remarkable claim Jesus made is the statement: "I am the truth." The following Scripture from the gospel of John, a recorded history of Jesus' life, gives important information on how to find truth.

What the Bible Tells Us

Jesus answered, "My teaching is not my own. It comes from him who sent me. If anyone chooses to do God's will, he will find out whether my teaching comes from God or whether I speak on my own. He who speaks on his own does so to gain honor for himself, but he who works for the honor of the one who sent him is a man of truth; there is nothing false about him." (John 7:16-18)

Jesus answered, "I am the way, the truth and the life. No one comes to the Father except through me." (John 14:6)

Note: As a human, Jesus lived during the time of the Roman empire. At the end of his ministry, he was accused of political treason by his countrymen. The following conversation took place as Jesus stood before the Roman governor, Pilate, during his trial.

Jesus said, "My kingdom is not of this world. If it were, my servants would fight to prevent my arrest by the Jews. But now my kingdom is from another place." "You are a king, then!" said Pilate. Jesus answered, "You are right in saying I am a king. In fact, for this reason I was born, and for this I came into the world, to testify to the truth. Everyone on the side of truth listens to me." "What is truth?" Pilate asked. (John 18:36-38a)

How the Bible Relates

1. How does Jesus assure us that he is telling the truth? What claims does he make about himself in John 7:16-18?

2. No leader of any major religious group has ever made the claims Jesus made in John 14:6. What do you think Jesus is saying about himself?

3. Why did Jesus come into the world?

4. Who listens to Jesus?

5. Can you identify with Pilate's final question to Jesus? What would you have asked Jesus?

The Bottom Line

Jesus not only points us to the truth, but he also embodies truth. If we wish to learn more about truth, we must learn more about Jesus.

Prayer

Dear God, in a world that promises so much but delivers so little, help us to find what is true and reliable. Amen.

A Final Word

I want you to know fully God's secret truth. That truth is Christ himself. And in him all the treasures of wisdom and knowledge are safely kept. (*The apostle Paul in Colossians 2:2-3,* New Century Version)

3: The Truth About Truth

Beginnings

When did you first discover that something you firmly believed in was actually false? For example, when did you find out that Santa Claus or Superman was only imaginary? How did you feel then? If possible, share a time when someone deceived you to the point that it had a major impact on your life.

What's Happening Today

We live in a time of universal distrust. We often find ourselves thinking that certain people are not telling us the truth. This includes not only used car salesmen but also politicians. A recent lead article in *Time* magazine states, "The public now assumes lying on the part of its representatives because it expects them to lie. . . . Politicians know that they are widely perceived as liars. It is no wonder that we listen to campaign promises with a 'grain of salt.'"

Other events feed our distrust. A young mother gains our overwhelming sympathy when she tells us that her young sons have been kidnapped, and then she admits drowning them strapped securely in the family car. Well-known celebrities deny committing heinous crimes but courts of law subsequently find them guilty.

Some religious leaders gain followers by convincing them to believe all that they say. Unfortunately, the truth surfaces too late and the world is riveted to news photos from places like Jonestown, Guyana, and Waco.

Who is telling the truth anymore? What can we believe? Is the tumor benign or malignant? Has the mechanic really fixed our car's brakes? Is our teenage son at the party as he said he would be?

In every area of life, we want to know the straight scoop; we don't want to waste our time with false promises. We want people to tell it like it is.

To know the truth in the realm of faith is vitally important. All religions lay claim to the truth, but which one should we believe? Which one is true? Sincerity of belief is not the issue. Many sincere people in the world believe lies. We are interested in reality and reliability.

When Jesus lived on earth, he made some astonishing statements and amazing claims. He often spoke of truth. In fact, he began most of his teachings by saying, "I tell you the truth. . . ." Perhaps the most remarkable claim Jesus made is the statement: "I am the truth." The following Scripture from the gospel of John, a recorded history of Jesus' life, gives important information on how to find truth.

What the Bible Tells Us

Jesus answered, "My teaching is not my own. It comes from him who sent me. If anyone chooses to do God's will, he will find out whether my teaching comes from God or whether I speak on my own. He who speaks on his own does so to gain honor for himself, but he who works for the honor of the one who sent him is a man of truth; there is nothing false about him." (John 7:16-18)

Jesus answered, "I am the way, the truth and the life. No one comes to the Father except through me." (John 14:6)

Note: As a human, Jesus lived during the time of the Roman empire. At the end of his ministry, he was accused of political treason by his countrymen. The following conversation took place as Jesus stood before the Roman governor, Pilate, during his trial.

Jesus said, "My kingdom is not of this world. If it were, my servants would fight to prevent my arrest by the Jews. But now my kingdom is from another place." "You are a king, then!" said Pilate. Jesus answered, "You are right in saying I am a king. In fact, for this reason I was born, and for this I came into the world, to testify to the truth. Everyone on the side of truth listens to me." "What is truth?" Pilate asked. (John 18:36-38a)

How the Bible Relates

1. How does Jesus assure us that he is telling the truth? What claims does he make about himself in John 7:16-18?

2. No leader of any major religious group has ever made the claims Jesus made in John 14:6. What do you think Jesus is saying about himself?

3. Why did Jesus come into the world?

4. Who listens to Jesus?

5. Can you identify with Pilate's final question to Jesus? What would you have asked Jesus?

The Bottom Line

Jesus not only points us to the truth, but he also embodies truth. If we wish to learn more about truth, we must learn more about Jesus.

Prayer

Dear God, in a world that promises so much but delivers so little, help us to find what is true and reliable. Amen.

A Final Word

I want you to know fully God's secret truth. That truth is Christ himself. And in him all the treasures of wisdom and knowledge are safely kept. *(The apostle Paul in Colossians 2:2-3, New Century Version)*

3: The Truth About Truth

Beginnings

When did you first discover that something you firmly believed in was actually false? For example, when did you find out that Santa Claus or Superman was only imaginary? How did you feel then? If possible, share a time when someone deceived you to the point that it had a major impact on your life.

What's Happening Today

We live in a time of universal distrust. We often find ourselves thinking that certain people are not telling us the truth. This includes not only used car salesmen but also politicians. A recent lead article in *Time* magazine states, "The public now assumes lying on the part of its representatives because it expects them to lie. . . . Politicians know that they are widely perceived as liars. It is no wonder that we listen to campaign promises with a 'grain of salt.'"

Other events feed our distrust. A young mother gains our overwhelming sympathy when she tells us that her young sons have been kidnapped, and then she admits drowning them strapped securely in the family car. Well-known celebrities deny committing heinous crimes but courts of law subsequently find them guilty.

Some religious leaders gain followers by convincing them to believe all that they say. Unfortunately, the truth surfaces too late and the world is riveted to news photos from places like Jonestown, Guyana, and Waco.

Who is telling the truth anymore? What can we believe? Is the tumor benign or malignant? Has the mechanic really fixed our car's brakes? Is our teenage son at the party as he said he would be?

In every area of life, we want to know the straight scoop; we don't want to waste our time with false promises. We want people to tell it like it is.

To know the truth in the realm of faith is vitally important. All religions lay claim to the truth, but which one should we believe? Which one is true? Sincerity of belief is not the issue. Many sincere people in the world believe lies. We are interested in reality and reliability.

When Jesus lived on earth, he made some astonishing statements and amazing claims. He often spoke of truth. In fact, he began most of his teachings by saying, "I tell you the truth. . . ." Perhaps the most remarkable claim Jesus made is the statement: "I am the truth." The following Scripture from the gospel of John, a recorded history of Jesus' life, gives important information on how to find truth.

What the Bible Tells Us

Jesus answered, "My teaching is not my own. It comes from him who sent me. If anyone chooses to do God's will, he will find out whether my teaching comes from God or whether I speak on my own. He who speaks on his own does so to gain honor for himself, but he who works for the honor of the one who sent him is a man of truth; there is nothing false about him." (John 7:16-18)

Jesus answered, "I am the way, the truth and the life. No one comes to the Father except through me." (John 14:6)

Note: As a human, Jesus lived during the time of the Roman empire. At the end of his ministry, he was accused of political treason by his countrymen. The following conversation took place as Jesus stood before the Roman governor, Pilate, during his trial.

Jesus said, "My kingdom is not of this world. If it were, my servants would fight to prevent my arrest by the Jews. But now my kingdom is from another place." "You are a king, then!" said Pilate. Jesus answered, "You are right in saying I am a king. In fact, for this reason I was born, and for this I came into the world, to testify to the truth. Everyone on the side of truth listens to me." "What is truth?" Pilate asked. (John 18:36-38a)

How the Bible Relates

1. How does Jesus assure us that he is telling the truth? What claims does he make about himself in John 7:16-18?

2. No leader of any major religious group has ever made the claims Jesus made in John 14:6. What do you think Jesus is saying about himself?

3. Why did Jesus come into the world?

4. Who listens to Jesus?

5. Can you identify with Pilate's final question to Jesus? What would you have asked Jesus?

The Bottom Line

Jesus not only points us to the truth, but he also embodies truth. If we wish to learn more about truth, we must learn more about Jesus.

Prayer

Dear God, in a world that promises so much but delivers so little, help us to find what is true and reliable. Amen.

A Final Word

I want you to know fully God's secret truth. That truth is Christ himself. And in him all the treasures of wisdom and knowledge are safely kept. (*The apostle Paul in Colossians 2:2-3, New Century Version*)

The Whole Truth and Nothing But the Truth

4: The Truth About Death

Introductory Notes

Death is not a popular subject in North America today. Eighty percent of American deaths occur in hospitals where the dying process is hidden from most people. Funeral homes have replaced the family home as the place for viewing the body, thereby hiding death from the public eye. Euphemisms such as "passed on," "laid to rest," and (in the case of animals) "put to sleep" promote denial of death.

Even for Christians, death is unattractive and unnatural. Because of Adam and Eve's disobedience, sin and death entered the world, making Christ's redemption necessary. He died so that both intruders—sin and death—would be completely conquered. Only by Christ's atonement has the sting of death been removed.

This session will deal with a subject that many people do not want to discuss. Some of your group members, however, may welcome the opportunity to express pain and fear. Allow them to share their experiences; you may express your feelings as well. Be careful not to sound "other-worldly." Although believers have a great and glorious hope, they also must watch others "walk through the valley of the shadow of death." Some day each of us will walk that valley, too.

During this session, you will acknowledge various perspectives of death, and then you can present the truth about the resurrection as expressed through the words of Jesus and the apostle Paul. Many people today glean much of their information from television, movies, and books. Some of that information is biblical, but much is highly speculative. In addition, the concept of reincarnation is growing more and more popular.

Also be sensitive to those in your group who may have lost a family member or friend recently. Their grief and pain may be too fresh to discuss openly. Some may be dealing with anger or guilt. Pray that God will give you the right words to say to them.

Pray too that God will use this lesson to challenge members of your group to prepare for their own deaths. Ask God for wisdom to listen to various viewpoints expressed by group members, but also to affirm the biblical truth about death. Again, be honest in admitting that much of what happens at death remains a mystery. Remind your group that this life, with all its imperfections, can be wonderful; so heaven, in all its perfection, has to be marvelous beyond imagination.

Beginning the Session

Greet your group members by name. Since the lesson topic may seem morbid and threatening to some, keep the initial conversation warm and light. Follow up on any concerns from the previous week. This is an important part of relationship building and shows you really *heard* the things they said—and cared enough to remember. At the same time, don't get sidetracked. Make sure each person has a copy of the Discussion Handout before you begin.

Beginnings

How do movies and TV either glamorize or minimize death? What part of death most frightens you? Why do you think most people are afraid to die?

Because this session may be difficult for some group members, begin with a more impersonal, nonthreatening question. After they've shared their thoughts on the media portrayals of death, move to the more personal level. Remembering the loss of a parent, a child, or even a family pet might produce great emotion. Questions may arise concerning the death of a pet. The Bible teaches that both humans and animals receive their life from God. The key difference is that animals were not created in the image of God as were the first humans (Genesis 1:27). Therefore, they are not the objects of God's redeeming love. While it may be that animals will play a role in the new heaven and earth, many questions remain. A simple answer, such as "I do not know for certain," is probably the best way to answer these questions.

If someone in your group has experienced a very painful loss recently, you might allow him or her to vent some of the pain. Sometimes this comes in the form of questioning God. Be careful not to come too quickly to God's defense; simply listening at this point might be more valuable. You might need to answer questions such as, "Why didn't God listen to my prayer?" or "Why did he allow my mother to die when I was ten?" with a statement like "I do not know why these things happen." Acknowledge their pain by saying something like, "It really hurts, doesn't it, when it seems like God doesn't care about our pain." Be very careful not to toss back with answers. People often are looking more for personal affirmation than answers.

You then might assert that these things happen to both good and bad people (Luke 13:1-5). When we deal with the death of someone we love, particularly if it is an accidental or premature death, we may feel that God is unloving or wishes to hurt us—or even that God is impotent and could not prevent it from happening. Scripture, however, indicates that God is a loving God who allows these things to happen for reasons we may never understand.

In the extended format, you may discuss why North American culture avoids confronting the reality of death. Is it because medical science seems to be able to prolong life? With new discoveries that help to prevent aging, do we think that we can effectively put off the inevitable?

What's Happening Today

Either you or someone in your group may read this section aloud. Allow time for discussion, but try to steer it in the direction of Jesus' words on the subject of death.

Your group members will perhaps recall some films or books on the subject. Acknowledge these without passing judgment at this point. Once again, be careful to separate a sometimes beautiful portrayal of death or the afterlife in a film or book from the truth as Scripture expresses it.

Stress that reliable information exists on this subject. Also point out that two differing explanations cannot be true at the same time. Reincarnation and the biblical teachings, for example, are not compatible. Certainly the idea that all awareness ceases with death does not agree with the teachings of Christianity. Some in your group may express different perspectives, but you can encourage them to at least consider what the Bible says about the subject.

What the Bible Tells Us

After you have read these passages aloud with your group, focus on the discussion questions that follow. Be prepared to answer questions about the context of these passages; some may not know why Jesus was on a cross or what happened after that, for example. Read the surrounding chapters beforehand to familiarize yourself with all the information you might need.

How the Bible Relates

1. What does Jesus say about himself?

This "I am" statement is one of seven found in the gospel of John. Jesus claimed to be the bread of life; the light of the world; the door; the good shepherd; the true vine; and finally, the way, the truth, and the life. These other "I am" statements are extremely significant, but Jesus' words in John 11 are absolutely remarkable. What Jesus claimed for himself has not been claimed by any other person in the history of the world. It is important that your group members understand how astounding his claim is. It's not just that eternal life comes through belief in Jesus. He also so embodies the idea of resurrection and new life that it's appropriate to say that he *is* the resurrection and the life.

You may need to explain Jesus' statement that "whoever lives and believes in me will never die." **Do you think that this means simply that anyone who believes in Jesus will never experience physical death? Might there be another kind of death that Jesus is referring to? If our bodies die, do you think that there can be a part of us that still lives on?** Obviously Jesus' statement cannot mean that his followers will not experience physical death. Rather, as one commentator has stated, "Death will have no eternal significance" for our spirit, our inner nature, will never die.

2. How do you think Martha felt about what Jesus was saying?

Martha must have been full of conflicted feelings as she ran to meet Jesus: anger, frustration, grief, impatience—and a bit of hope. Martha had heard stories of Jesus' raising the dead to life. A young girl, for example, had been brought back to life by Jesus' hand (Luke 8:40-56). Could he possibly have enough power over death to do the same for Lazarus? This question must have been on Martha's mind.

 In the extended session, you'll have time to share some of the background of this story with your group. Even without this background, however, your group can work through the following questions: **What did Jesus say about Lazarus? How did Martha interpret Jesus' statement? How did Jesus expand on his meaning?**

Martha was looking for a short-term miracle: the raising of her brother from death. Jesus eventually did this! **But what greater miracle did he promise? How does this miracle show God's power over death more completely and victoriously? Which is a temporary solution, and which is forever? How might it be possible to live even though one dies physically? Who will experience this life, according to Jesus?** Hopefully your group will begin to understand the concept of eternal life as they work through these questions.

 In the extended format, you might discuss whether eternal life occurs only in the future or if it begins when a person believes in Christ. Jesus teaches the latter. With this understanding, death becomes the passageway from one life to another life. **How might this truth change the way a person lives right now?**

3. What does Jesus promise to the criminal who is being crucified with him? What do you think Jesus means?

Once again, Jesus promises something rather amazing. Regardless of the criminal's past life, his current trust in Christ would allow him to enter into heaven. You might mention that the criminal at least had the opportunity to observe the way that Jesus was dying. He had heard Jesus asking God to forgive those who were crucifying him. The robber could see that Jesus was no ordinary man. **How was the second criminal's attitude different from that of the first? How did he respond to Jesus? In light** of Jesus' statement to Martha, why do you think Jesus promised him eternal life in paradise?

Note: Tyndale's commentary indicates that the word "paradise" comes from the Persian word meaning "garden." It was used as a description for the Garden of Eden. In Bible times, it referred to a place of eternal happiness in the world to come.

4. To what action does the Bible compare death and burial?

Associating the idea of planting a seed with burying a body is extremely appropriate. **When you look at an unfamiliar seed, can you tell what kind of plant or flower it will produce? Why? How is that similar to what happens when a person dies? How does this idea make you feel—comforted, curious, skeptical? Why?** In the same way that it's hard to imagine the beautiful flower or plant that will spring from a particular seed, so it's difficult for us to imagine what our resurrected bodies will look like. Even the process of bringing a decomposed or cremated body back to life is beyond our comprehension.

These verses should be comforting to your group. We struggle with our physical bodies now. Illness, injury, fatigue, physical handicaps—all these limit our dreams, goals, desires. **What would life be like if we had none of these limitations?** Again, it's hard to imagine; but we can't help sensing that it may really be true. Perhaps this teaching will be most meaningful to group members who have severe physical limitations or who have close family members who do.

5. What do these verses tell us about life after death?

Avoid speculation concerning the nature of our bodies in the afterlife. The Bible reveals relatively little information on this subject, except for that contained in the accounts of Jesus' appearances after his resurrection. We do know that Jesus' body had changed enough that his friends did not easily recognize him. John 20 says that Jesus appeared in a room with closed and locked doors. The nail prints in his hands and the spear wound in his side were evident. Though his appearance and the nature of his body had changed, he was not what some people would call a ghost. He ate food with his disciples, and he invited Thomas to touch him (John 20:27).

The following questions might be helpful for your group to consider as they discuss this question: **What are some of the ways in which the Bible contrasts a dead body with the new, resurrected one?** Look at the terms that describe our present bodies: *dying, decaying, sick, embarrassing, weak, human.* Then look at the words that describe the new bodies: *full of glory, full of strength, super-human, supernatural, spiritual.*

How does this perspective change the fear of death? How might the funeral of a Christian be different from that of a person who does not believe in Christ? An aide in a nursing home recently became a Christian. When the hope of eternal life was explained to her, her face lit up.

"Well, that explains it!" she said. "Usually when someone here dies, a lot of cursing and swearing and anger goes on. But these Christians, when they die, the family seems so at peace and content with things. I could never figure out why!" You might share this story with your group and ask about their own experiences. **Have you ever attended a Christian funeral? Was there any mention of the hope of life after death and the resurrection? Did any hope mix with the grief?** Again, be very sensitive here to group members who may have recently experienced the death of someone they loved—especially if that person was not a Christian and died without this hope.

The Bottom Line

We're concerned about how we die—but our most important question is "What will happen after death?" Some people believe that after death there is a permanent unconsciousness—a nothingness. Some believe they come back to earth in various forms until they "get it right." Jesus says to those who believe in him, "Today you will be with me in paradise."

As you discuss "The Bottom Line" with your group, mention that Jesus' words "I am the resurrection and the life" are not simply an interesting philosophical statement. They are the truth that God asks us to receive and then to act upon. Ultimately, this is what you want to happen in the lives of your group members. Remember, however, that this may take some time. Do not push those who are not ready to accept this truth. As he proclaimed the hope of the resurrection before the council at Athens (Acts 17), the apostle Paul faced three different reactions—sneers, further questions, and belief. You likely will too.

Optional Prayer Time

Lead your group through this prayer if you feel it's appropriate to your discussion. Add your own prayer for needs that group members have expressed in your discussion today. Ask for God's healing love to touch the lives of group members who have said they are struggling with the loss of a loved one.

Prayer

Dear Lord, the thought of death fills us with pain and fear. Take both of these away. Amen.

A Final Word

Our earthly bodies, the ones we have now that can die, must be transformed into heavenly bodies that cannot perish but will live forever. When this happens, then at last this Scripture will come true—"Death is swallowed up in victory." O death, where then your victory? Where then your sting? (*The apostle Paul in 1 Corinthians 15:53-55, The Living Bible*)

4: The Truth About Death

Introductory Notes

Death is not a popular subject in North America today. Eighty percent of American deaths occur in hospitals where the dying process is hidden from most people. Funeral homes have replaced the family home as the place for viewing the body, thereby hiding death from the public eye. Euphemisms such as "passed on," "laid to rest," and (in the case of animals) "put to sleep" promote denial of death.

Even for Christians, death is unattractive and unnatural. Because of Adam and Eve's disobedience, sin and death entered the world, making Christ's redemption necessary. He died so that both intruders—sin and death—would be completely conquered. Only by Christ's atonement has the sting of death been removed.

This session will deal with a subject that many people do not want to discuss. Some of your group members, however, may welcome the opportunity to express pain and fear. Allow them to share their experiences; you may express your feelings as well. Be careful not to sound "other-worldly." Although believers have a great and glorious hope, they also must watch others "walk through the valley of the shadow of death." Some day each of us will walk that valley, too.

During this session, you will acknowledge various perspectives of death, and then you can present the truth about the resurrection as expressed through the words of Jesus and the apostle Paul. Many people today glean much of their information from television, movies, and books. Some of that information is biblical, but much is highly speculative. In addition, the concept of reincarnation is growing more and more popular.

Also be sensitive to those in your group who may have lost a family member or friend recently. Their grief and pain may be too fresh to discuss openly. Some may be dealing with anger or guilt. Pray that God will give you the right words to say to them.

Pray too that God will use this lesson to challenge members of your group to prepare for their own deaths. Ask God for wisdom to listen to various viewpoints expressed by group members, but also to affirm the biblical truth about death. Again, be honest in admitting that much of what happens at death remains a mystery. Remind your group that this life, with all its imperfections, can be wonderful; so heaven, in all its perfection, has to be marvelous beyond imagination.

Beginning the Session

Greet your group members by name. Since the lesson topic may seem morbid and threatening to some, keep the initial conversation warm and light. Follow up on any concerns from the previous week. This is an important part of relationship building and shows you really *heard* the things they said—and cared enough to remember. At the same time, don't get sidetracked. Make sure each person has a copy of the Discussion Handout before you begin.

Beginnings

How do movies and TV either glamorize or minimize death? What part of death most frightens you? Why do you think most people are afraid to die?

Because this session may be difficult for some group members, begin with a more impersonal, nonthreatening question. After they've shared their thoughts on the media portrayals of death, move to the more personal level. Remembering the loss of a parent, a child, or even a family pet might produce great emotion. Questions may arise concerning the death of a pet. The Bible teaches that both humans and animals receive their life from God. The key difference is that animals were not created in the image of God as were the first humans (Genesis 1:27). Therefore, they are not the objects of God's redeeming love. While it may be that animals will play a role in the new heaven and earth, many questions remain. A simple answer, such as "I do not know for certain," is probably the best way to answer these questions.

If someone in your group has experienced a very painful loss recently, you might allow him or her to vent some of the pain. Sometimes this comes in the form of questioning God. Be careful not to come too quickly to God's defense; simply listening at this point might be more valuable. You might need to answer questions such as, "Why didn't God listen to my prayer?" or "Why did he allow my mother to die when I was ten?" with a statement like "I do not know why these things happen." Acknowledge their pain by saying something like, "It really hurts, doesn't it, when it seems like God doesn't care about our pain." Be very careful not to toss back with answers. People often are looking more for personal affirmation than answers.

You then might assert that these things happen to both good and bad people (Luke 13:1-5). When we deal with the death of someone we love, particularly if it is an accidental or premature death, we may feel that God is unloving or wishes to hurt us—or even that God is impotent and could not prevent it from happening. Scripture, however, indicates that God is a loving God who allows these things to happen for reasons we may never understand.

In the extended format, you may discuss why North American culture avoids confronting the reality of death. Is it because medical science seems to be able to prolong life? With new discoveries that help to prevent aging, do we think that we can effectively put off the inevitable?

What's Happening Today

Either you or someone in your group may read this section aloud. Allow time for discussion, but try to steer it in the direction of Jesus' words on the subject of death.

Your group members will perhaps recall some films or books on the subject. Acknowledge these without passing judgment at this point. Once again, be careful to separate a sometimes beautiful portrayal of death or the afterlife in a film or book from the truth as Scripture expresses it.

Stress that reliable information exists on this subject. Also point out that two differing explanations cannot be true at the same time. Reincarnation and the biblical teachings, for example, are not compatible. Certainly the idea that all awareness ceases with death does not agree with the teachings of Christianity. Some in your group may express different perspectives, but you can encourage them to at least consider what the Bible says about the subject.

What the Bible Tells Us

After you have read these passages aloud with your group, focus on the discussion questions that follow. Be prepared to answer questions about the context of these passages; some may not know why Jesus was on a cross or what happened after that, for example. Read the surrounding chapters beforehand to familiarize yourself with all the information you might need.

How the Bible Relates

1. What does Jesus say about himself?

This "I am" statement is one of seven found in the gospel of John. Jesus claimed to be the bread of life; the light of the world; the door; the good shepherd; the true vine; and finally, the way, the truth, and the life. These other "I am" statements are extremely significant, but Jesus' words in John 11 are absolutely remarkable. What Jesus claimed for himself has not been claimed by any other person in the history of the world. It is important that your group members understand how astounding his claim is. It's not just that eternal life comes through belief in Jesus. He also so embodies the idea of resurrection and new life that it's appropriate to say that he *is* the resurrection and the life.

You may need to explain Jesus' statement that "whoever lives and believes in me will never die." **Do you think that this means simply that anyone who believes**

in Jesus will never experience physical death? Might there be another kind of death that Jesus is referring to? If our bodies die, do you think that there can be a part of us that still lives on?** Obviously Jesus' statement cannot mean that his followers will not experience physical death. Rather, as one commentator has stated, "Death will have no eternal significance" for our spirit, our inner nature, will never die.

2. How do you think Martha felt about what Jesus was saying?

Martha must have been full of conflicted feelings as she ran to meet Jesus: anger, frustration, grief, impatience—and a bit of hope. Martha had heard stories of Jesus' raising the dead to life. A young girl, for example, had been brought back to life by Jesus' hand (Luke 8:40-56). Could he possibly have enough power over death to do the same for Lazarus? This question must have been on Martha's mind.

 In the extended session, you'll have time to share some of the background of this story with your group. Even without this background, however, your group can work through the following questions: **What did Jesus say about Lazarus? How did Martha interpret Jesus' statement? How did Jesus expand on his meaning?**

Martha was looking for a short-term miracle: the raising of her brother from death. Jesus eventually did this! **But what greater miracle did he promise? How does this miracle show God's power over death more completely and victoriously? Which is a temporary solution, and which is forever? How might it be possible to live even though one dies physically? Who will experience this life, according to Jesus?** Hopefully your group will begin to understand the concept of eternal life as they work through these questions.

 In the extended format, you might discuss whether eternal life occurs only in the future or if it begins when a person believes in Christ. Jesus teaches the latter. With this understanding, death becomes the passageway from one life to another life. **How might this truth change the way a person lives right now?**

3. What does Jesus promise to the criminal who is being crucified with him? What do you think Jesus means?

Once again, Jesus promises something rather amazing. Regardless of the criminal's past life, his current trust in Christ would allow him to enter into heaven. You might mention that the criminal at least had the opportunity to observe the way that Jesus was dying. He had heard Jesus asking God to forgive those who were crucifying him. The robber could see that Jesus was no ordinary man. **How was the second criminal's attitude different from that of the first? How did he respond to Jesus? In light** of Jesus' statement to Martha, why do you think Jesus promised him eternal life in paradise?

Note: Tyndale's commentary indicates that the word "paradise" comes from the Persian word meaning "garden." It was used as a description for the Garden of Eden. In Bible times, it referred to a place of eternal happiness in the world to come.

4. To what action does the Bible compare death and burial?

Associating the idea of planting a seed with burying a body is extremely appropriate. **When you look at an unfamiliar seed, can you tell what kind of plant or flower it will produce? Why? How is that similar to what happens when a person dies? How does this idea make you feel—comforted, curious, skeptical? Why?** In the same way that it's hard to imagine the beautiful flower or plant that will spring from a particular seed, so it's difficult for us to imagine what our resurrected bodies will look like. Even the process of bringing a decomposed or cremated body back to life is beyond our comprehension.

These verses should be comforting to your group. We struggle with our physical bodies now. Illness, injury, fatigue, physical handicaps—all these limit our dreams, goals, desires. **What would life be like if we had none of these limitations?** Again, it's hard to imagine; but we can't help sensing that it may really be true. Perhaps this teaching will be most meaningful to group members who have severe physical limitations or who have close family members who do.

5. What do these verses tell us about life after death?

Avoid speculation concerning the nature of our bodies in the afterlife. The Bible reveals relatively little information on this subject, except for that contained in the accounts of Jesus' appearances after his resurrection. We do know that Jesus' body had changed enough that his friends did not easily recognize him. John 20 says that Jesus appeared in a room with closed and locked doors. The nail prints in his hands and the spear wound in his side were evident. Though his appearance and the nature of his body had changed, he was not what some people would call a ghost. He ate food with his disciples, and he invited Thomas to touch him (John 20:27).

The following questions might be helpful for your group to consider as they discuss this question: **What are some of the ways in which the Bible contrasts a dead body with the new, resurrected one?** Look at the terms that describe our present bodies: *dying, decaying, sick, embarrassing, weak, human.* Then look at the words that describe the new bodies: *full of glory, full of strength, superhuman, supernatural, spiritual.*

How does this perspective change the fear of death? How might the funeral of a Christian be different from that of a person who does not believe in Christ? An aide in a nursing home recently became a Christian. When the hope of eternal life was explained to her, her face lit up.

"Well, that explains it!" she said. "Usually when someone here dies, a lot of cursing and swearing and anger goes on. But these Christians, when they die, the family seems so at peace and content with things. I could never figure out why!" You might share this story with your group and ask about their own experiences. **Have you ever attended a Christian funeral? Was there any mention of the hope of life after death and the resurrection? Did any hope mix with the grief?** Again, be very sensitive here to group members who may have recently experienced the death of someone they loved—especially if that person was not a Christian and died without this hope.

The Bottom Line

We're concerned about how we die—but our most important question is "What will happen after death?" Some people believe that after death there is a permanent unconsciousness—a nothingness. Some believe they come back to earth in various forms until they "get it right." Jesus says to those who believe in him, "Today you will be with me in paradise."

As you discuss "The Bottom Line" with your group, mention that Jesus' words "I am the resurrection and the life" are not simply an interesting philosophical statement. They are the truth that God asks us to receive and then to act upon. Ultimately, this is what you want to happen in the lives of your group members. Remember, however, that this may take some time. Do not push those who are not ready to accept this truth. As he proclaimed the hope of the resurrection before the council at Athens (Acts 17), the apostle Paul faced three different reactions—sneers, further questions, and belief. You likely will too.

Optional Prayer Time

Lead your group through this prayer if you feel it's appropriate to your discussion. Add your own prayer for needs that group members have expressed in your discussion today. Ask for God's healing love to touch the lives of group members who have said they are struggling with the loss of a loved one.

Prayer

Dear Lord, the thought of death fills us with pain and fear. Take both of these away. Amen.

A Final Word

Our earthly bodies, the ones we have now that can die, must be transformed into heavenly bodies that cannot perish but will live forever. When this happens, then at last this Scripture will come true—"Death is swallowed up in victory." O death, where then your victory? Where then your sting? *(The apostle Paul in 1 Corinthians 15:53-55, The Living Bible)*

4: The Truth About Death

Beginnings

How do movies and TV either glamorize or minimize death? What part of death most frightens you? Why do you think most people are afraid to die?

What's Happening Today

Over the past few years, the book and movie industries have produced some popular titles on the subject of death. Some have portrayed the death of a spouse or lover—and then showed that person returning as a ghost to assist the former partner to move away from grief and into a new life. Others trace the dying process. Some violent movies glorify death, while violent cartoons feature characters who are indestructible.

How We Die, a best-selling book written by a physician, chronicles in detail the physiological process by which many people die. Other books deal with the same theme but use a psychological or spiritual framework.

People are afraid of death. We fear other things too, of course. Fear of public speaking, fear of heights, and fear of flying are high on the "greatest phobias" list. Perhaps we repress our fear of death, assuming that "it won't happen to me" or that it will happen in the distant future.

Some people who claim near-death experiences describe death as a pleasant experience. Many mention the sensation of a bright light or of travel through a tunnel. People continue to remain perplexed, however, about what happens after death. Some believe in reincarnation; others contend that once this life ends, humans live on only if their organs have been donated to another person. Still others feel that their lives continue through their children. Many people believe that physical death ends any conscious awareness.

Can we know anything for certain about death? Yes. Only one person among the world's religious leaders has died and been brought back to life—and later was seen alive by hundreds of eyewitnesses. That person is Jesus. Both his death and his resurrection are amply and historically documented. So Jesus' teachings on death are very significant.

What the Bible Tells Us

Many Jews had come to Martha and Mary to comfort them in the loss of their brother. When Martha heard that Jesus was coming, she went out to meet him, but Mary stayed at home.

"Lord," Martha said to Jesus, "if you had been here, my brother would not have died. But I know that even now God will give you whatever you ask."

Jesus said to her, "Your brother will rise again."

Martha answered, "I know he will rise again in the resurrection at the last day."

Jesus said to her, "I am the resurrection and the life. He who believes in me will live, even though he dies; and whoever lives and believes in me will never die. Do you believe this?" (John 11:19-26)

They crucified Jesus, along with the criminals—one on his right, the other on his left. . . .

One of the criminals who hung there hurled insults at [Jesus]: "Aren't you the Christ? Save yourself and us!"

But the other criminal rebuked him. "Don't you fear God," he said, "since you are under the same sentence? We are punished justly, for we are getting what our deeds deserve. But this man has done nothing wrong."

Then he said, "Jesus, remember me when you come into your kingdom."

Jesus answered him, "I tell you the truth, today you will be with me in paradise." (Luke 23:39-43)

Someone may ask, "How will the dead be brought back to life again? What kind of bodies will they have?" What a foolish question! You will find the answer in your own garden! When you put a seed into the ground it doesn't grow into a plant unless it 'dies' first. And when the green shoot comes up out of the seed, it is very different from the seed you first planted. . . .

In the same way, our earthly bodies which die and decay are different from the bodies we shall have when we come back to life again, for they will never die. The bodies we have now embarrass

*us for they become sick and die; but they will be full of glory when we
come back to life again. Yes, they are weak, dying bodies now, but when
we live again they will be full of strength. They are just human bodies at
death, but when they come back to life they will be superhuman bodies.*
(1 Corinthians 15:35-37, 42-44, The Living Bible)

How the Bible Relates

1. What does Jesus say about himself?

2. How do you think Martha felt about what Jesus was saying?

3. What does Jesus promise to the criminal who is being crucified
   with him? What do you think Jesus means?

4. To what action does the Bible compare death and burial?

5. What do these verses tell us about life after death?

The Bottom Line

We're concerned about how we die—but our most important
question is "What will happen after death?" Some people believe
that after death there is a permanent unconsciousness—a nothingness. Some believe they come back to earth in various forms until
they "get it right." Jesus says to those who believe in him, "Today
you will be with me in paradise."

Prayer

Dear Lord, the thought of death fills us with pain and fear.
Take both of these away. Amen.

A Final Word

Our earthly bodies, the ones we have now that can die, must be
transformed into heavenly bodies that cannot perish but will live
forever. When this happens, then at last this Scripture will come
true—"Death is swallowed up in victory." O death, where then
your victory? Where then your sting? *(The apostle Paul in
1 Corinthians 15:53-55, The Living Bible)*

4: The Truth About Death

Beginnings

How do movies and TV either glamorize or minimize death? What part of death most frightens you? Why do you think most people are afraid to die?

What's Happening Today

Over the past few years, the book and movie industries have produced some popular titles on the subject of death. Some have portrayed the death of a spouse or lover—and then showed that person returning as a ghost to assist the former partner to move away from grief and into a new life. Others trace the dying process. Some violent movies glorify death, while violent cartoons feature characters who are indestructible.

How We Die, a best-selling book written by a physician, chronicles in detail the physiological process by which many people die. Other books deal with the same theme but use a psychological or spiritual framework.

People are afraid of death. We fear other things too, of course. Fear of public speaking, fear of heights, and fear of flying are high on the "greatest phobias" list. Perhaps we repress our fear of death, assuming that "it won't happen to me" or that it will happen in the distant future.

Some people who claim near-death experiences describe death as a pleasant experience. Many mention the sensation of a bright light or of travel through a tunnel. People continue to remain perplexed, however, about what happens after death. Some believe in reincarnation; others contend that once this life ends, humans live on only if their organs have been donated to another person. Still others feel that their lives continue through their children. Many people believe that physical death ends any conscious awareness.

Can we know anything for certain about death? Yes. Only one person among the world's religious leaders has died and been brought back to life—and later was seen alive by hundreds of eyewitnesses. That person is Jesus. Both his death and his resurrection are amply and historically documented. So Jesus' teachings on death are very significant.

What the Bible Tells Us

Many Jews had come to Martha and Mary to comfort them in the loss of their brother. When Martha heard that Jesus was coming, she went out to meet him, but Mary stayed at home.

"Lord," Martha said to Jesus, "if you had been here, my brother would not have died. But I know that even now God will give you whatever you ask."

Jesus said to her, "Your brother will rise again."

Martha answered, "I know he will rise again in the resurrection at the last day."

Jesus said to her, "I am the resurrection and the life. He who believes in me will live, even though he dies; and whoever lives and believes in me will never die. Do you believe this?" (John 11:19-26)

They crucified Jesus, along with the criminals—one on his right, the other on his left. . . .

One of the criminals who hung there hurled insults at [Jesus]: "Aren't you the Christ? Save yourself and us!"

But the other criminal rebuked him. "Don't you fear God," he said, "since you are under the same sentence? We are punished justly, for we are getting what our deeds deserve. But this man has done nothing wrong."

Then he said, "Jesus, remember me when you come into your kingdom."

Jesus answered him, "I tell you the truth, today you will be with me in paradise." (Luke 23:39-43)

Someone may ask, "How will the dead be brought back to life again? What kind of bodies will they have?" What a foolish question! You will find the answer in your own garden! When you put a seed into the ground it doesn't grow into a plant unless it 'dies' first. And when the green shoot comes up out of the seed, it is very different from the seed you first planted. . . .

In the same way, our earthly bodies which die and decay are different from the bodies we shall have when we come back to life again, for they will never die. The bodies we have now embarrass

*us for they become sick and die; but they will be full of glory when we
come back to life again. Yes, they are weak, dying bodies now, but when
we live again they will be full of strength. They are just human bodies at
death, but when they come back to life they will be superhuman bodies.*
(1 Corinthians 15:35-37, 42-44, The Living Bible)

How the Bible Relates

1. What does Jesus say about himself?

2. How do you think Martha felt about what Jesus was saying?

3. What does Jesus promise to the criminal who is being crucified
   with him? What do you think Jesus means?

4. To what action does the Bible compare death and burial?

5. What do these verses tell us about life after death?

The Bottom Line

We're concerned about how we die—but our most important
question is "What will happen after death?" Some people believe
that after death there is a permanent unconsciousness—a nothingness. Some believe they come back to earth in various forms until
they "get it right." Jesus says to those who believe in him, "Today
you will be with me in paradise."

Prayer

Dear Lord, the thought of death fills us with pain and fear.
Take both of these away. Amen.

A Final Word

Our earthly bodies, the ones we have now that can die, must be
transformed into heavenly bodies that cannot perish but will live
forever. When this happens, then at last this Scripture will come
true—"Death is swallowed up in victory." O death, where then
your victory? Where then your sting? *(The apostle Paul in
1 Corinthians 15:53-55, The Living Bible)*

4: The Truth About Death

Beginnings

How do movies and TV either glamorize or minimize death? What part of death most frightens you? Why do you think most people are afraid to die?

What's Happening Today

Over the past few years, the book and movie industries have produced some popular titles on the subject of death. Some have portrayed the death of a spouse or lover—and then showed that person returning as a ghost to assist the former partner to move away from grief and into a new life. Others trace the dying process. Some violent movies glorify death, while violent cartoons feature characters who are indestructible.

How We Die, a best-selling book written by a physician, chronicles in detail the physiological process by which many people die. Other books deal with the same theme but use a psychological or spiritual framework.

People are afraid of death. We fear other things too, of course. Fear of public speaking, fear of heights, and fear of flying are high on the "greatest phobias" list. Perhaps we repress our fear of death, assuming that "it won't happen to me" or that it will happen in the distant future.

Some people who claim near-death experiences describe death as a pleasant experience. Many mention the sensation of a bright light or of travel through a tunnel. People continue to remain perplexed, however, about what happens after death. Some believe in reincarnation; others contend that once this life ends, humans live on only if their organs have been donated to another person. Still others feel that their lives continue through their children. Many people believe that physical death ends any conscious awareness.

Can we know anything for certain about death? Yes. Only one person among the world's religious leaders has died and been brought back to life—and later was seen alive by hundreds of eyewitnesses. That person is Jesus. Both his death and his resurrection are amply and historically documented. So Jesus' teachings on death are very significant.

What the Bible Tells Us

Many Jews had come to Martha and Mary to comfort them in the loss of their brother. When Martha heard that Jesus was coming, she went out to meet him, but Mary stayed at home.

"Lord," Martha said to Jesus, "if you had been here, my brother would not have died. But I know that even now God will give you whatever you ask."

Jesus said to her, "Your brother will rise again."

Martha answered, "I know he will rise again in the resurrection at the last day."

Jesus said to her, "I am the resurrection and the life. He who believes in me will live, even though he dies; and whoever lives and believes in me will never die. Do you believe this?" (John 11:19-26)

They crucified Jesus, along with the criminals—one on his right, the other on his left. . . .

One of the criminals who hung there hurled insults at [Jesus]: "Aren't you the Christ? Save yourself and us!"

But the other criminal rebuked him. "Don't you fear God," he said, "since you are under the same sentence? We are punished justly, for we are getting what our deeds deserve. But this man has done nothing wrong."

Then he said, "Jesus, remember me when you come into your kingdom."

Jesus answered him, "I tell you the truth, today you will be with me in paradise." (Luke 23:39-43)

Someone may ask, "How will the dead be brought back to life again? What kind of bodies will they have?" What a foolish question! You will find the answer in your own garden! When you put a seed into the ground it doesn't grow into a plant unless it 'dies' first. And when the green shoot comes up out of the seed, it is very different from the seed you first planted. . . .

In the same way, our earthly bodies which die and decay are different from the bodies we shall have when we come back to life again, for they will never die. The bodies we have now embarrass

us for they become sick and die; but they will be full of glory when we come back to life again. Yes, they are weak, dying bodies now, but when we live again they will be full of strength. They are just human bodies at death, but when they come back to life they will be superhuman bodies. (1 Corinthians 15:35-37, 42-44, The Living Bible)

How the Bible Relates

1. What does Jesus say about himself?

2. How do you think Martha felt about what Jesus was saying?

3. What does Jesus promise to the criminal who is being crucified with him? What do you think Jesus means?

4. To what action does the Bible compare death and burial?

5. What do these verses tell us about life after death?

The Bottom Line

We're concerned about how we die—but our most important question is "What will happen after death?" Some people believe that after death there is a permanent unconsciousness—a nothingness. Some believe they come back to earth in various forms until they "get it right." Jesus says to those who believe in him, "Today you will be with me in paradise."

Prayer

Dear Lord, the thought of death fills us with pain and fear. Take both of these away. Amen.

A Final Word

Our earthly bodies, the ones we have now that can die, must be transformed into heavenly bodies that cannot perish but will live forever. When this happens, then at last this Scripture will come true—"Death is swallowed up in victory." O death, where then your victory? Where then your sting? *(The apostle Paul in 1 Corinthians 15:53-55, The Living Bible)*

4: The Truth About Death

Beginnings

How do movies and TV either glamorize or minimize death? What part of death most frightens you? Why do you think most people are afraid to die?

What's Happening Today

Over the past few years, the book and movie industries have produced some popular titles on the subject of death. Some have portrayed the death of a spouse or lover—and then showed that person returning as a ghost to assist the former partner to move away from grief and into a new life. Others trace the dying process. Some violent movies glorify death, while violent cartoons feature characters who are indestructible.

How We Die, a best-selling book written by a physician, chronicles in detail the physiological process by which many people die. Other books deal with the same theme but use a psychological or spiritual framework.

People are afraid of death. We fear other things too, of course. Fear of public speaking, fear of heights, and fear of flying are high on the "greatest phobias" list. Perhaps we repress our fear of death, assuming that "it won't happen to me" or that it will happen in the distant future.

Some people who claim near-death experiences describe death as a pleasant experience. Many mention the sensation of a bright light or of travel through a tunnel. People continue to remain perplexed, however, about what happens after death. Some believe in reincarnation; others contend that once this life ends, humans live on only if their organs have been donated to another person. Still others feel that their lives continue through their children. Many people believe that physical death ends any conscious awareness.

Can we know anything for certain about death? Yes. Only one person among the world's religious leaders has died and been brought back to life—and later was seen alive by hundreds of eyewitnesses. That person is Jesus. Both his death and his resurrection are amply and historically documented. So Jesus' teachings on death are very significant.

What the Bible Tells Us

Many Jews had come to Martha and Mary to comfort them in the loss of their brother. When Martha heard that Jesus was coming, she went out to meet him, but Mary stayed at home.

"Lord," Martha said to Jesus, "if you had been here, my brother would not have died. But I know that even now God will give you whatever you ask."

Jesus said to her, "Your brother will rise again."

Martha answered, "I know he will rise again in the resurrection at the last day."

Jesus said to her, "I am the resurrection and the life. He who believes in me will live, even though he dies; and whoever lives and believes in me will never die. Do you believe this?" (John 11:19-26)

They crucified Jesus, along with the criminals—one on his right, the other on his left. . . .

One of the criminals who hung there hurled insults at [Jesus]: "Aren't you the Christ? Save yourself and us!"

But the other criminal rebuked him. "Don't you fear God," he said, "since you are under the same sentence? We are punished justly, for we are getting what our deeds deserve. But this man has done nothing wrong."

Then he said, "Jesus, remember me when you come into your kingdom."

Jesus answered him, "I tell you the truth, today you will be with me in paradise." (Luke 23:39-43)

Someone may ask, "How will the dead be brought back to life again? What kind of bodies will they have?" What a foolish question! You will find the answer in your own garden! When you put a seed into the ground it doesn't grow into a plant unless it 'dies' first. And when the green shoot comes up out of the seed, it is very different from the seed you first planted. . . .

In the same way, our earthly bodies which die and decay are different from the bodies we shall have when we come back to life again, for they will never die. The bodies we have now embarrass

*us for they become sick and die; but they will be full of glory when we
come back to life again. Yes, they are weak, dying bodies now, but when
we live again they will be full of strength. They are just human bodies at
death, but when they come back to life they will be superhuman bodies.*
(1 Corinthians 15:35-37, 42-44, The Living Bible)

How the Bible Relates

1. What does Jesus say about himself?

2. How do you think Martha felt about what Jesus was saying?

3. What does Jesus promise to the criminal who is being crucified
   with him? What do you think Jesus means?

4. To what action does the Bible compare death and burial?

5. What do these verses tell us about life after death?

The Bottom Line

We're concerned about how we die—but our most important
question is "What will happen after death?" Some people believe
that after death there is a permanent unconsciousness—a nothingness. Some believe they come back to earth in various forms until
they "get it right." Jesus says to those who believe in him, "Today
you will be with me in paradise."

Prayer

Dear Lord, the thought of death fills us with pain and fear.
Take both of these away. Amen.

A Final Word

Our earthly bodies, the ones we have now that can die, must be
transformed into heavenly bodies that cannot perish but will live
forever. When this happens, then at last this Scripture will come
true—"Death is swallowed up in victory." O death, where then
your victory? Where then your sting? *(The apostle Paul in
1 Corinthians 15:53-55, The Living Bible)*

4: The Truth About Death

Beginnings

How do movies and TV either glamorize or minimize death? What part of death most frightens you? Why do you think most people are afraid to die?

What's Happening Today

Over the past few years, the book and movie industries have produced some popular titles on the subject of death. Some have portrayed the death of a spouse or lover—and then showed that person returning as a ghost to assist the former partner to move away from grief and into a new life. Others trace the dying process. Some violent movies glorify death, while violent cartoons feature characters who are indestructible.

How We Die, a best-selling book written by a physician, chronicles in detail the physiological process by which many people die. Other books deal with the same theme but use a psychological or spiritual framework.

People are afraid of death. We fear other things too, of course. Fear of public speaking, fear of heights, and fear of flying are high on the "greatest phobias" list. Perhaps we repress our fear of death, assuming that "it won't happen to me" or that it will happen in the distant future.

Some people who claim near-death experiences describe death as a pleasant experience. Many mention the sensation of a bright light or of travel through a tunnel. People continue to remain perplexed, however, about what happens after death. Some believe in reincarnation; others contend that once this life ends, humans live on only if their organs have been donated to another person. Still others feel that their lives continue through their children. Many people believe that physical death ends any conscious awareness.

Can we know anything for certain about death? Yes. Only one person among the world's religious leaders has died and been brought back to life—and later was seen alive by hundreds of eyewitnesses. That person is Jesus. Both his death and his resurrection are amply and historically documented. So Jesus' teachings on death are very significant.

What the Bible Tells Us

Many Jews had come to Martha and Mary to comfort them in the loss of their brother. When Martha heard that Jesus was coming, she went out to meet him, but Mary stayed at home.

"Lord," Martha said to Jesus, "if you had been here, my brother would not have died. But I know that even now God will give you whatever you ask."

Jesus said to her, "Your brother will rise again."

Martha answered, "I know he will rise again in the resurrection at the last day."

Jesus said to her, "I am the resurrection and the life. He who believes in me will live, even though he dies; and whoever lives and believes in me will never die. Do you believe this?" (John 11:19-26)

They crucified Jesus, along with the criminals—one on his right, the other on his left. . . .

One of the criminals who hung there hurled insults at [Jesus]: "Aren't you the Christ? Save yourself and us!"

But the other criminal rebuked him. "Don't you fear God," he said, "since you are under the same sentence? We are punished justly, for we are getting what our deeds deserve. But this man has done nothing wrong."

Then he said, "Jesus, remember me when you come into your kingdom."

Jesus answered him, "I tell you the truth, today you will be with me in paradise." (Luke 23:39-43)

Someone may ask, "How will the dead be brought back to life again? What kind of bodies will they have?" What a foolish question! You will find the answer in your own garden! When you put a seed into the ground it doesn't grow into a plant unless it 'dies' first. And when the green shoot comes up out of the seed, it is very different from the seed you first planted. . . .

In the same way, our earthly bodies which die and decay are different from the bodies we shall have when we come back to life again, for they will never die. The bodies we have now embarrass

us for they become sick and die; but they will be full of glory when we
come back to life again. Yes, they are weak, dying bodies now, but when
we live again they will be full of strength. They are just human bodies at
death, but when they come back to life they will be superhuman bodies.
(1 Corinthians 15:35-37, 42-44, The Living Bible)

How the Bible Relates

1. What does Jesus say about himself?

2. How do you think Martha felt about what Jesus was saying?

3. What does Jesus promise to the criminal who is being crucified with him? What do you think Jesus means?

4. To what action does the Bible compare death and burial?

5. What do these verses tell us about life after death?

The Bottom Line

We're concerned about how we die—but our most important question is "What will happen after death?" Some people believe that after death there is a permanent unconsciousness—a nothingness. Some believe they come back to earth in various forms until they "get it right." Jesus says to those who believe in him, "Today you will be with me in paradise."

Prayer

Dear Lord, the thought of death fills us with pain and fear. Take both of these away. Amen.

A Final Word

Our earthly bodies, the ones we have now that can die, must be transformed into heavenly bodies that cannot perish but will live forever. When this happens, then at last this Scripture will come true—"Death is swallowed up in victory." O death, where then your victory? Where then your sting? *(The apostle Paul in 1 Corinthians 15:53-55, The Living Bible)*

4: The Truth About Death

Beginnings

How do movies and TV either glamorize or minimize death? What part of death most frightens you? Why do you think most people are afraid to die?

What's Happening Today

Over the past few years, the book and movie industries have produced some popular titles on the subject of death. Some have portrayed the death of a spouse or lover—and then showed that person returning as a ghost to assist the former partner to move away from grief and into a new life. Others trace the dying process. Some violent movies glorify death, while violent cartoons feature characters who are indestructible.

How We Die, a best-selling book written by a physician, chronicles in detail the physiological process by which many people die. Other books deal with the same theme but use a psychological or spiritual framework.

People are afraid of death. We fear other things too, of course. Fear of public speaking, fear of heights, and fear of flying are high on the "greatest phobias" list. Perhaps we repress our fear of death, assuming that "it won't happen to me" or that it will happen in the distant future.

Some people who claim near-death experiences describe death as a pleasant experience. Many mention the sensation of a bright light or of travel through a tunnel. People continue to remain perplexed, however, about what happens after death. Some believe in reincarnation; others contend that once this life ends, humans live on only if their organs have been donated to another person. Still others feel that their lives continue through their children. Many people believe that physical death ends any conscious awareness.

Can we know anything for certain about death? Yes. Only one person among the world's religious leaders has died and been brought back to life—and later was seen alive by hundreds of eyewitnesses. That person is Jesus. Both his death and his resurrection are amply and historically documented. So Jesus' teachings on death are very significant.

What the Bible Tells Us

Many Jews had come to Martha and Mary to comfort them in the loss of their brother. When Martha heard that Jesus was coming, she went out to meet him, but Mary stayed at home.

"Lord," Martha said to Jesus, "if you had been here, my brother would not have died. But I know that even now God will give you whatever you ask."

Jesus said to her, "Your brother will rise again."

Martha answered, "I know he will rise again in the resurrection at the last day."

Jesus said to her, "I am the resurrection and the life. He who believes in me will live, even though he dies; and whoever lives and believes in me will never die. Do you believe this?" (John 11:19-26)

They crucified Jesus, along with the criminals—one on his right, the other on his left. . . .

One of the criminals who hung there hurled insults at [Jesus]: "Aren't you the Christ? Save yourself and us!"

But the other criminal rebuked him. "Don't you fear God," he said, "since you are under the same sentence? We are punished justly, for we are getting what our deeds deserve. But this man has done nothing wrong."

Then he said, "Jesus, remember me when you come into your kingdom."

Jesus answered him, "I tell you the truth, today you will be with me in paradise." (Luke 23:39-43)

Someone may ask, "How will the dead be brought back to life again? What kind of bodies will they have?" What a foolish question! You will find the answer in your own garden! When you put a seed into the ground it doesn't grow into a plant unless it 'dies' first. And when the green shoot comes up out of the seed, it is very different from the seed you first planted. . . .

In the same way, our earthly bodies which die and decay are different from the bodies we shall have when we come back to life again, for they will never die. The bodies we have now embarrass

us for they become sick and die; but they will be full of glory when we
come back to life again. Yes, they are weak, dying bodies now, but when
we live again they will be full of strength. They are just human bodies at
death, but when they come back to life they will be superhuman bodies.
(1 Corinthians 15:35-37, 42-44, The Living Bible)

How the Bible Relates

1. What does Jesus say about himself?

2. How do you think Martha felt about what Jesus was saying?

3. What does Jesus promise to the criminal who is being crucified with him? What do you think Jesus means?

4. To what action does the Bible compare death and burial?

5. What do these verses tell us about life after death?

The Bottom Line

We're concerned about how we die—but our most important question is "What will happen after death?" Some people believe that after death there is a permanent unconsciousness—a nothingness. Some believe they come back to earth in various forms until they "get it right." Jesus says to those who believe in him, "Today you will be with me in paradise."

Prayer

Dear Lord, the thought of death fills us with pain and fear. Take both of these away. Amen.

A Final Word

Our earthly bodies, the ones we have now that can die, must be transformed into heavenly bodies that cannot perish but will live forever. When this happens, then at last this Scripture will come true—"Death is swallowed up in victory." O death, where then your victory? Where then your sting? *(The apostle Paul in*
1 Corinthians 15:53-55, The Living Bible)

4: The Truth About Death

Beginnings

How do movies and TV either glamorize or minimize death? What part of death most frightens you? Why do you think most people are afraid to die?

What's Happening Today

Over the past few years, the book and movie industries have produced some popular titles on the subject of death. Some have portrayed the death of a spouse or lover—and then showed that person returning as a ghost to assist the former partner to move away from grief and into a new life. Others trace the dying process. Some violent movies glorify death, while violent cartoons feature characters who are indestructible.

How We Die, a best-selling book written by a physician, chronicles in detail the physiological process by which many people die. Other books deal with the same theme but use a psychological or spiritual framework.

People are afraid of death. We fear other things too, of course. Fear of public speaking, fear of heights, and fear of flying are high on the "greatest phobias" list. Perhaps we repress our fear of death, assuming that "it won't happen to me" or that it will happen in the distant future.

Some people who claim near-death experiences describe death as a pleasant experience. Many mention the sensation of a bright light or of travel through a tunnel. People continue to remain perplexed, however, about what happens after death. Some believe in reincarnation; others contend that once this life ends, humans live on only if their organs have been donated to another person. Still others feel that their lives continue through their children. Many people believe that physical death ends any conscious awareness.

Can we know anything for certain about death? Yes. Only one person among the world's religious leaders has died and been brought back to life—and later was seen alive by hundreds of eyewitnesses. That person is Jesus. Both his death and his resurrection are amply and historically documented. So Jesus' teachings on death are very significant.

What the Bible Tells Us

Many Jews had come to Martha and Mary to comfort them in the loss of their brother. When Martha heard that Jesus was coming, she went out to meet him, but Mary stayed at home.

"Lord," Martha said to Jesus, "if you had been here, my brother would not have died. But I know that even now God will give you whatever you ask."

Jesus said to her, "Your brother will rise again."

Martha answered, "I know he will rise again in the resurrection at the last day."

Jesus said to her, "I am the resurrection and the life. He who believes in me will live, even though he dies; and whoever lives and believes in me will never die. Do you believe this?" (John 11:19-26)

They crucified Jesus, along with the criminals—one on his right, the other on his left. . . .

One of the criminals who hung there hurled insults at [Jesus]: "Aren't you the Christ? Save yourself and us!"

But the other criminal rebuked him. "Don't you fear God," he said, "since you are under the same sentence? We are punished justly, for we are getting what our deeds deserve. But this man has done nothing wrong."

Then he said, "Jesus, remember me when you come into your kingdom."

Jesus answered him, "I tell you the truth, today you will be with me in paradise." (Luke 23:39-43)

Someone may ask, "How will the dead be brought back to life again? What kind of bodies will they have?" What a foolish question! You will find the answer in your own garden! When you put a seed into the ground it doesn't grow into a plant unless it 'dies' first. And when the green shoot comes up out of the seed, it is very different from the seed you first planted. . . .

In the same way, our earthly bodies which die and decay are different from the bodies we shall have when we come back to life again, for they will never die. The bodies we have now embarrass

us for they become sick and die; but they will be full of glory when we come back to life again. Yes, they are weak, dying bodies now, but when we live again they will be full of strength. They are just human bodies at death, but when they come back to life they will be superhuman bodies.
(1 Corinthians 15:35-37, 42-44, The Living Bible)

How the Bible Relates

1. What does Jesus say about himself?

2. How do you think Martha felt about what Jesus was saying?

3. What does Jesus promise to the criminal who is being crucified with him? What do you think Jesus means?

4. To what action does the Bible compare death and burial?

5. What do these verses tell us about life after death?

The Bottom Line

We're concerned about how we die—but our most important question is "What will happen after death?" Some people believe that after death there is a permanent unconsciousness—a nothingness. Some believe they come back to earth in various forms until they "get it right." Jesus says to those who believe in him, "Today you will be with me in paradise."

Prayer

Dear Lord, the thought of death fills us with pain and fear. Take both of these away. Amen.

A Final Word

Our earthly bodies, the ones we have now that can die, must be transformed into heavenly bodies that cannot perish but will live forever. When this happens, then at last this Scripture will come true—"Death is swallowed up in victory." O death, where then your victory? Where then your sting? *(The apostle Paul in 1 Corinthians 15:53-55, The Living Bible)*

4: The Truth About Death

Beginnings

How do movies and TV either glamorize or minimize death? What part of death most frightens you? Why do you think most people are afraid to die?

What's Happening Today

Over the past few years, the book and movie industries have produced some popular titles on the subject of death. Some have portrayed the death of a spouse or lover—and then showed that person returning as a ghost to assist the former partner to move away from grief and into a new life. Others trace the dying process. Some violent movies glorify death, while violent cartoons feature characters who are indestructible.

How We Die, a best-selling book written by a physician, chronicles in detail the physiological process by which many people die. Other books deal with the same theme but use a psychological or spiritual framework.

People are afraid of death. We fear other things too, of course. Fear of public speaking, fear of heights, and fear of flying are high on the "greatest phobias" list. Perhaps we repress our fear of death, assuming that "it won't happen to me" or that it will happen in the distant future.

Some people who claim near-death experiences describe death as a pleasant experience. Many mention the sensation of a bright light or of travel through a tunnel. People continue to remain perplexed, however, about what happens after death. Some believe in reincarnation; others contend that once this life ends, humans live on only if their organs have been donated to another person. Still others feel that their lives continue through their children. Many people believe that physical death ends any conscious awareness.

Can we know anything for certain about death? Yes. Only one person among the world's religious leaders has died and been brought back to life—and later was seen alive by hundreds of eyewitnesses. That person is Jesus. Both his death and his resurrection are amply and historically documented. So Jesus' teachings on death are very significant.

What the Bible Tells Us

Many Jews had come to Martha and Mary to comfort them in the loss of their brother. When Martha heard that Jesus was coming, she went out to meet him, but Mary stayed at home.

"Lord," Martha said to Jesus, "if you had been here, my brother would not have died. But I know that even now God will give you whatever you ask."

Jesus said to her, "Your brother will rise again."

Martha answered, "I know he will rise again in the resurrection at the last day."

Jesus said to her, "I am the resurrection and the life. He who believes in me will live, even though he dies; and whoever lives and believes in me will never die. Do you believe this?" (John 11:19-26)

They crucified Jesus, along with the criminals—one on his right, the other on his left. . . .

One of the criminals who hung there hurled insults at [Jesus]: "Aren't you the Christ? Save yourself and us!"

But the other criminal rebuked him. "Don't you fear God," he said, "since you are under the same sentence? We are punished justly, for we are getting what our deeds deserve. But this man has done nothing wrong."

Then he said, "Jesus, remember me when you come into your kingdom."

Jesus answered him, "I tell you the truth, today you will be with me in paradise." (Luke 23:39-43)

Someone may ask, "How will the dead be brought back to life again? What kind of bodies will they have?" What a foolish question! You will find the answer in your own garden! When you put a seed into the ground it doesn't grow into a plant unless it 'dies' first. And when the green shoot comes up out of the seed, it is very different from the seed you first planted. . . .

In the same way, our earthly bodies which die and decay are different from the bodies we shall have when we come back to life again, for they will never die. The bodies we have now embarrass

us for they become sick and die; but they will be full of glory when we come back to life again. Yes, they are weak, dying bodies now, but when we live again they will be full of strength. They are just human bodies at death, but when they come back to life they will be superhuman bodies.
(1 Corinthians 15:35-37, 42-44, The Living Bible)

How the Bible Relates

1. What does Jesus say about himself?

2. How do you think Martha felt about what Jesus was saying?

3. What does Jesus promise to the criminal who is being crucified with him? What do you think Jesus means?

4. To what action does the Bible compare death and burial?

5. What do these verses tell us about life after death?

The Bottom Line

We're concerned about how we die—but our most important question is "What will happen after death?" Some people believe that after death there is a permanent unconsciousness—a nothingness. Some believe they come back to earth in various forms until they "get it right." Jesus says to those who believe in him, "Today you will be with me in paradise."

Prayer

Dear Lord, the thought of death fills us with pain and fear. Take both of these away. Amen.

A Final Word

Our earthly bodies, the ones we have now that can die, must be transformed into heavenly bodies that cannot perish but will live forever. When this happens, then at last this Scripture will come true—"Death is swallowed up in victory." O death, where then your victory? Where then your sting? *(The apostle Paul in 1 Corinthians 15:53-55, The Living Bible)*

4: The Truth About Death

Beginnings

How do movies and TV either glamorize or minimize death? What part of death most frightens you? Why do you think most people are afraid to die?

What's Happening Today

Over the past few years, the book and movie industries have produced some popular titles on the subject of death. Some have portrayed the death of a spouse or lover—and then showed that person returning as a ghost to assist the former partner to move away from grief and into a new life. Others trace the dying process. Some violent movies glorify death, while violent cartoons feature characters who are indestructible.

How We Die, a best-selling book written by a physician, chronicles in detail the physiological process by which many people die. Other books deal with the same theme but use a psychological or spiritual framework.

People are afraid of death. We fear other things too, of course. Fear of public speaking, fear of heights, and fear of flying are high on the "greatest phobias" list. Perhaps we repress our fear of death, assuming that "it won't happen to me" or that it will happen in the distant future.

Some people who claim near-death experiences describe death as a pleasant experience. Many mention the sensation of a bright light or of travel through a tunnel. People continue to remain perplexed, however, about what happens after death. Some believe in reincarnation; others contend that once this life ends, humans live on only if their organs have been donated to another person. Still others feel that their lives continue through their children. Many people believe that physical death ends any conscious awareness.

Can we know anything for certain about death? Yes. Only one person among the world's religious leaders has died and been brought back to life—and later was seen alive by hundreds of eyewitnesses. That person is Jesus. Both his death and his resurrection are amply and historically documented. So Jesus' teachings on death are very significant.

What the Bible Tells Us

Many Jews had come to Martha and Mary to comfort them in the loss of their brother. When Martha heard that Jesus was coming, she went out to meet him, but Mary stayed at home.

"Lord," Martha said to Jesus, "if you had been here, my brother would not have died. But I know that even now God will give you whatever you ask."

Jesus said to her, "Your brother will rise again."

Martha answered, "I know he will rise again in the resurrection at the last day."

Jesus said to her, "I am the resurrection and the life. He who believes in me will live, even though he dies; and whoever lives and believes in me will never die. Do you believe this?" (John 11:19-26)

They crucified Jesus, along with the criminals—one on his right, the other on his left. . . .

One of the criminals who hung there hurled insults at [Jesus]: "Aren't you the Christ? Save yourself and us!"

But the other criminal rebuked him. "Don't you fear God," he said, "since you are under the same sentence? We are punished justly, for we are getting what our deeds deserve. But this man has done nothing wrong."

Then he said, "Jesus, remember me when you come into your kingdom."

Jesus answered him, "I tell you the truth, today you will be with me in paradise." (Luke 23:39-43)

Someone may ask, "How will the dead be brought back to life again? What kind of bodies will they have?" What a foolish question! You will find the answer in your own garden! When you put a seed into the ground it doesn't grow into a plant unless it 'dies' first. And when the green shoot comes up out of the seed, it is very different from the seed you first planted. . . .

In the same way, our earthly bodies which die and decay are different from the bodies we shall have when we come back to life again, for they will never die. The bodies we have now embarrass

us for they become sick and die; but they will be full of glory when we
come back to life again. Yes, they are weak, dying bodies now, but when
we live again they will be full of strength. They are just human bodies at
death, but when they come back to life they will be superhuman bodies.
(1 Corinthians 15:35-37, 42-44, The Living Bible)

How the Bible Relates

1. What does Jesus say about himself?

2. How do you think Martha felt about what Jesus was saying?

3. What does Jesus promise to the criminal who is being crucified
   with him? What do you think Jesus means?

4. To what action does the Bible compare death and burial?

5. What do these verses tell us about life after death?

The Bottom Line

We're concerned about how we die—but our most important
question is "What will happen after death?" Some people believe
that after death there is a permanent unconsciousness—a nothingness. Some believe they come back to earth in various forms until
they "get it right." Jesus says to those who believe in him, "Today
you will be with me in paradise."

Prayer

Dear Lord, the thought of death fills us with pain and fear.
Take both of these away. Amen.

A Final Word

Our earthly bodies, the ones we have now that can die, must be
transformed into heavenly bodies that cannot perish but will live
forever. When this happens, then at last this Scripture will come
true—"Death is swallowed up in victory." O death, where then
your victory? Where then your sting? *(The apostle Paul in*
1 Corinthians 15:53-55, The Living Bible)

4: The Truth About Death

Beginnings

How do movies and TV either glamorize or minimize death? What part of death most frightens you? Why do you think most people are afraid to die?

What's Happening Today

Over the past few years, the book and movie industries have produced some popular titles on the subject of death. Some have portrayed the death of a spouse or lover—and then showed that person returning as a ghost to assist the former partner to move away from grief and into a new life. Others trace the dying process. Some violent movies glorify death, while violent cartoons feature characters who are indestructible.

How We Die, a best-selling book written by a physician, chronicles in detail the physiological process by which many people die. Other books deal with the same theme but use a psychological or spiritual framework.

People are afraid of death. We fear other things too, of course. Fear of public speaking, fear of heights, and fear of flying are high on the "greatest phobias" list. Perhaps we repress our fear of death, assuming that "it won't happen to me" or that it will happen in the distant future.

Some people who claim near-death experiences describe death as a pleasant experience. Many mention the sensation of a bright light or of travel through a tunnel. People continue to remain perplexed, however, about what happens after death. Some believe in reincarnation; others contend that once this life ends, humans live on only if their organs have been donated to another person. Still others feel that their lives continue through their children. Many people believe that physical death ends any conscious awareness.

Can we know anything for certain about death? Yes. Only one person among the world's religious leaders has died and been brought back to life—and later was seen alive by hundreds of eyewitnesses. That person is Jesus. Both his death and his resurrection are amply and historically documented. So Jesus' teachings on death are very significant.

What the Bible Tells Us

Many Jews had come to Martha and Mary to comfort them in the loss of their brother. When Martha heard that Jesus was coming, she went out to meet him, but Mary stayed at home.

"Lord," Martha said to Jesus, "if you had been here, my brother would not have died. But I know that even now God will give you whatever you ask."

Jesus said to her, "Your brother will rise again."

Martha answered, "I know he will rise again in the resurrection at the last day."

Jesus said to her, "I am the resurrection and the life. He who believes in me will live, even though he dies; and whoever lives and believes in me will never die. Do you believe this?" (John 11:19-26)

They crucified Jesus, along with the criminals—one on his right, the other on his left. . . .

One of the criminals who hung there hurled insults at [Jesus]: "Aren't you the Christ? Save yourself and us!"

But the other criminal rebuked him. "Don't you fear God," he said, "since you are under the same sentence? We are punished justly, for we are getting what our deeds deserve. But this man has done nothing wrong."

Then he said, "Jesus, remember me when you come into your kingdom."

Jesus answered him, "I tell you the truth, today you will be with me in paradise." (Luke 23:39-43)

Someone may ask, "How will the dead be brought back to life again? What kind of bodies will they have?" What a foolish question! You will find the answer in your own garden! When you put a seed into the ground it doesn't grow into a plant unless it 'dies' first. And when the green shoot comes up out of the seed, it is very different from the seed you first planted. . . .

In the same way, our earthly bodies which die and decay are different from the bodies we shall have when we come back to life again, for they will never die. The bodies we have now embarrass

us for they become sick and die; but they will be full of glory when we come back to life again. Yes, they are weak, dying bodies now, but when we live again they will be full of strength. They are just human bodies at death, but when they come back to life they will be superhuman bodies. (1 Corinthians 15:35-37, 42-44, The Living Bible)

How the Bible Relates

1. What does Jesus say about himself?

2. How do you think Martha felt about what Jesus was saying?

3. What does Jesus promise to the criminal who is being crucified with him? What do you think Jesus means?

4. To what action does the Bible compare death and burial?

5. What do these verses tell us about life after death?

The Bottom Line

We're concerned about how we die—but our most important question is "What will happen after death?" Some people believe that after death there is a permanent unconsciousness—a nothingness. Some believe they come back to earth in various forms until they "get it right." Jesus says to those who believe in him, "Today you will be with me in paradise."

Prayer

Dear Lord, the thought of death fills us with pain and fear. Take both of these away. Amen.

A Final Word

Our earthly bodies, the ones we have now that can die, must be transformed into heavenly bodies that cannot perish but will live forever. When this happens, then at last this Scripture will come true—"Death is swallowed up in victory." O death, where then your victory? Where then your sting? *(The apostle Paul in 1 Corinthians 15:53-55, The Living Bible)*

The Whole Truth and Nothing But the Truth

5: The Truth About Humanity

Introductory Notes

The topic for this session may seem to be removed from group members' everyday lives. Most probably have not thought about it much, but it has much to do with how they live, treat others, and interact with the world around them.

In fact, your members' views on what it means to be human will affect every aspect of their life. Do they believe that human life is an accident, that our lives are a passing spark snuffed out at death? Do they consider humans to be a species of animal, without a distinct purpose or moral responsibility? Do they assume if God exists, he takes little interest in who we are or what we do?

These perspectives are common in our society. They affect how we deal with others, how we treat our earth, and how we hold ourselves accountable for our actions. These views affect our own self-image and our relationship with God.

The Bible clearly places human beings in a special part of God's created world. It explains the glory and the beauty of being human—as well as the ugliness and meanness that pervades human nature. When we study the Bible, we come to understand the mystery of our nature—glory and shame mixed together. It paves the way for the "good news" message: We have fallen short, but we can regain what we have lost through God's love and the death of his Son.

Allow your group members to wrestle with the concepts presented in the passages from Genesis and Romans. They may not like these ideas, or they may reject them as outdated and naive. Challenge them to explore the fuller meaning of this teaching: how it affects our relationships to each other and the earth. Encourage them to consider what the Bible says about sin and how we were made to live differently.

As you prepare, pray for your group members' increased understanding and spiritual awareness. Ask the Spirit, who was present at creation, to hover over your group as you study these Scriptures together. Depend on the Spirit's prompting to ask the right questions and give helpful answers. Pray that you may be part of bringing into being another "new creation"—that of a person made new by faith in Jesus Christ.

Beginning the Session

Welcome your group members enthusiastically, asking how their week has gone and following up on situations they've mentioned during previous sessions. Always allow for a few minutes of "connecting" time in which members can exchange greetings, questions, and conversation. Nurture the supportive nature of this group, even when you have limited time for study.

When everyone has had a chance to join in the opening conversation, hand out the discussion sheets and get them focused on the beginning questions.

Beginnings

What is the best thing you can think of about being a man? A woman? What is the worst thing about it? We live on a planet with millions of other kinds of living creatures. Major differences separate humans and other living creatures. What are these differences?

After distributing the discussion sheets, read these questions aloud to your group and give time for their responses. They may need a few minutes to pull their minds away from daily schedules, pressures, and activities, but encourage them to step back from all that long enough to think about some basic questions of our existence: Where do we come from? Why are we here?

 In the longer format, you may want to explore with the group some viewpoints on human nature suggested by psychologists, scientists, and others. For example, many scientists regard the human species as simply another form of animal life, evolved from a simple cell structure over millions of years. Some sociologists see humans as products of their environments; others claim that no moral laws bind us as humans. Find out what your group members have heard and what they think. Try to listen more than you talk. Lead this discussion into a reading of "What's Happening Today."

What's Happening Today

After reading this section aloud, ask for responses before moving on to the Scripture reading and discussion questions. Keep this response time brief, since you will want to leave ample time for the questions.

What the Bible Tells Us

Read the passages from Genesis and Romans to your group or invite a group member to read. It should be obvious to your group, but you may want to clarify that God is referring to all humanity and not simply the male sex when he says, "Let us make man in our image." Briefly answer any questions group members ask about any other words or phrases.

How the Bible Relates

1. In whose image were people made, according to the Bible? What do you think this means?

As you begin your discussion, clarify that the Bible assumes two things: (1) God exists, and (2) God created the universe and everything in it. Though your group members may not agree with these two points, ask them to set aside their questions for now and simply accept that these beliefs are basic to understanding the Bible.

The Bible says that something unique happened when God created human beings. **How did God distinguish between humans and other creatures? What did God give to humans that he gave to no other creature?** Two things should become clear: Humans were created to "rule . . . over all the earth," and they were created by God "in his own image." Both clearly distinguish between humans and any other living creature.

Look more closely at the phrase "in his image." **Which characteristics of God do you think he may have given humans? What qualities set us apart from other living creatures? Might these differences be present because humans have been made "in the image of God"?** Allow group members to think about these questions and to wrestle with how humans might reflect some of the qualities of God.

The Scriptures do not explain "in his image" more specifically here, though other places hint of its meaning. For now, it is sufficient to establish that human beings have a special place in creation because they reflect some part of God's nature that animals do not.

 You might explore this a bit more in the longer format: **What makes you different from an animal? What qualities do you possess that a dog or horse or cat does not? How are human relationships different from those among animals or between animals and humans?** These questions will help group members focus on those special qualities that God has given them.

You may want to look at one more aspect of the image of God: "male and female he created them." The preceding verse says "in the image of God he created him, male and female. . . ." **What does this suggest about God? Though we speak of God as "he" or "him," how might "male and female" reflect God's image and likeness?** Affirm that while God is a spirit and neither male nor female, the best qualities of both male and female originate in God, who created them both.

Members may ask about the word "our" in relationship to God ("in our image," "our likeness"). They might wonder if that means that there is more than one God. The Bible speaks of one true and living God, who has revealed himself in three persons: Father, Son, and Holy Spirit. This is a mystery of the Christian faith, something that no one can fully understand or explain, but which must simply be accepted in faith.

2. What was their job description?

This may be an eye-opener for some group members. **What role do human beings play, compared with all other creatures? How far does human rule extend? What do you think God means by "rule"?** Use these questions to help your members see that humans enjoy an almost godlike position on earth, with the job of overseeing all other creatures. But God's words indicate that he has in mind more of a caring servanthood than a tyranny that exploits the world for its own desires and whims.

 In the longer format, relate God's command to some of the situations we face. **How might this translate into some of today's environmental issues?** This should lead naturally into the next discussion question.

3. How might this perspective affect how we treat each other and our world?

You've already touched on how God has intended us to treat our world. Explore this in more detail, if you wish; but be sure also to deal with how God expects us to treat each other.

As you do so, consider the following questions: **What are some ways that our society views people? How can you "use" another person (or part of the earth's resources) for your own purposes? How does that happen in our society?** Your group should have a lot to talk about here. Many of the problems that our society faces today—rising crime, spouse and child abuse, teenage pregnancy, poverty issues—have their roots in how people see each other. If we see others only as means to an end or as objects that help us to achieve our own goals and desires, then we have lost a respect for each other's rights and dignity.

Without that respect, crime is easy. Studies show that the most hardened criminals are those who failed to bond with a parent or authority figure. They have never learned to love and respect another person.

But that's not all. Not only do we not respect others, but we also do not respect ourselves. Many people consider themselves useless, worthless, and hopeless. **How does that perspective affect a person's life? How does the Bible's account of our beginnings give us a different view of ourselves? What difference might that make to someone who suffers from a broken and hopeless view of his or her existence?**

How do you think God intended us to treat each other, in light of this passage? Use this question to affirm again the goodness in relationships—respect, love, and care—that comprise healthy relationships.

4. According to Romans, what do all people have in common?

At this point, your group will begin to deal with the question "What went wrong with God's good plan?" You might look first at the phrase "all have sinned." **What is** sin? **Is sin only great and terrible wrongs, or is it also small, everyday wrongs?** Sit back and listen to your group members talk about sin.

Many people today think that "sin" refers only to terrible atrocities—mass murders, Hitler-type violence, and so on. But the Bible looks at sin in a simpler, broader way. To Christians, sin means simply "missing the mark." In other words, it's failing to live how God intended us to live. **What does the Genesis passage tell us about how God intended us to live? How have we missed that mark?** Your discussion of broken relationships and a scarred creation should quickly point up the undeniable presence of sin in all of our lives. Be as specific as you can to help group members understand the power and impact of sin.

 In the longer format, briefly retell the story of Adam and Eve's disobedience in the Garden of Eden for group members who may be unfamiliar with it. Help them realize that humans were created perfect and splendid—and then, because of their own wrongdoing, became marred and stained with sin.

Because of sin, we all "fall short of the glory of God." **What is "glory"?** Webster describes the word "glory" as "praise, honor, or distinction . . . something that secures praise or renown . . . great beauty or splendor . . . something marked by beauty and resplendence." **What kind of glory were people created to have, according to Genesis 1? How have they fallen short of this?** These questions should merely reinforce what your group members have been discovering throughout this discussion: God created us to fulfill a splendid and beautiful role in his creation—and human society today certainly does not reflect what God had intended it to be.

Imagine what God's glory might be like. If you wish, read a few verses from the Psalms (e.g., Psalm 89:5-8; 96; 97:1-6) or from Isaiah 40 that describe God's glory and majesty. **How can someone who lies or cheats or steals or hurts others share in that glory?** As it stands, no one can. That's the bad news.

But the good news—that's what the word "gospel" means—is this: God offers to make everything right again. Let your group know that God has not left things to stand as they are, hopelessly mired in sin. The next session will deal with the good news of the gospel message. Whet group members' appetite for hearing that good news by referring to it briefly here.

 In the longer format, you will have time to explore this more fully, especially if you sense that some group members are ready to hear and respond to the good news of God's love and forgiveness in Jesus.

5. In your experience, does the Bible's teaching on human nature seem true? Why or why not?

Use this time to listen to what your group members have learned from this session. Don't give them the impression that you're looking for "right" answers here; encourage them to explore their own questions and struggles honestly. If some hold different views from those of Genesis and Romans, it may take a long time for them to change those basic and fundamental beliefs. Encourage them to explore the Bible's perspective honestly and thoroughly.

The Bottom Line

The Bible gives us good news and bad news. The good news is this: All people have been created in God's likeness, with a great potential for doing good on this earth. The bad news is that the image of God in us is completely tarnished because of sin. But more good news follows the bad: God offers us a way to get back all we've lost.

Read through the "Bottom Line" with your group and again affirm that God has offered each of us a way to regain all that we've lost: a restored friendship with God, healed relationships with each other, a rebuilding of God's qualities and character within us, and the ability to restore and work with God's creation.

Optional Prayer Time

Ask for needs for which group members would like prayer during the week. Follow up on earlier concerns and make a mental note of anything shared that may call for a card of encouragement, a phone call to say "How are you doing?" or a meal or other tangible expression of help during this week.

Prayer

Dear God, help me to take time in my busyness to think about where I came from and what you intend my life to be. Help me to honestly face areas of wrongdoing in my life and to look to you for help. Amen.

A Final Word

O Lord our God, the majesty and glory of your name fills all the earth and overflows the heavens. When I look up into the night skies and see the work of your fingers—the moon and stars you have made—I cannot understand how you can bother with mere puny man, to pay any attention to him! And yet you have made him only a little lower than the angels, and placed a crown of glory and honor upon his head. You have put him in charge of everything you made. *(David in Psalm 8:1, 3-6, The Living Bible)*

5: The Truth About Humanity

Introductory Notes

The topic for this session may seem to be removed from group members' everyday lives. Most probably have not thought about it much, but it has much to do with how they live, treat others, and interact with the world around them.

In fact, your members' views on what it means to be human will affect every aspect of their life. Do they believe that human life is an accident, that our lives are a passing spark snuffed out at death? Do they consider humans to be a species of animal, without a distinct purpose or moral responsibility? Do they assume if God exists, he takes little interest in who we are or what we do?

These perspectives are common in our society. They affect how we deal with others, how we treat our earth, and how we hold ourselves accountable for our actions. These views affect our own self-image and our relationship with God.

The Bible clearly places human beings in a special part of God's created world. It explains the glory and the beauty of being human—as well as the ugliness and meanness that pervades human nature. When we study the Bible, we come to understand the mystery of our nature—glory and shame mixed together. It paves the way for the "good news" message: We have fallen short, but we can regain what we have lost through God's love and the death of his Son.

Allow your group members to wrestle with the concepts presented in the passages from Genesis and Romans. They may not like these ideas, or they may reject them as outdated and naive. Challenge them to explore the fuller meaning of this teaching: how it affects our relationships to each other and the earth. Encourage them to consider what the Bible says about sin and how we were made to live differently.

As you prepare, pray for your group members' increased understanding and spiritual awareness. Ask the Spirit, who was present at creation, to hover over your group as you study these Scriptures together. Depend on the Spirit's prompting to ask the right questions and give helpful answers. Pray that you may be part of bringing into being another "new creation"—that of a person made new by faith in Jesus Christ.

Beginning the Session

Welcome your group members enthusiastically, asking how their week has gone and following up on situations they've mentioned during previous sessions. Always allow for a few minutes of "connecting" time in which members can exchange greetings, questions, and conversation. Nurture the supportive nature of this group, even when you have limited time for study.

When everyone has had a chance to join in the opening conversation, hand out the discussion sheets and get them focused on the beginning questions.

Beginnings

What is the best thing you can think of about being a man? A woman? What is the worst thing about it? We live on a planet with millions of other kinds of living creatures. Major differences separate humans and other living creatures. What are these differences?

After distributing the discussion sheets, read these questions aloud to your group and give time for their responses. They may need a few minutes to pull their minds away from daily schedules, pressures, and activities, but encourage them to step back from all that long enough to think about some basic questions of our existence: Where do we come from? Why are we here?

 In the longer format, you may want to explore with the group some viewpoints on human nature suggested by psychologists, scientists, and others. For example, many scientists regard the human species as simply another form of animal life, evolved from a simple cell structure over millions of years. Some sociologists see humans as products of their environments; others claim that no moral laws bind us as humans. Find out what your group members have heard and what they think. Try to listen more than you talk. Lead this discussion into a reading of "What's Happening Today."

What's Happening Today

After reading this section aloud, ask for responses before moving on to the Scripture reading and discussion questions. Keep this response time brief, since you will want to leave ample time for the questions.

What the Bible Tells Us

Read the passages from Genesis and Romans to your group or invite a group member to read. It should be obvious to your group, but you may want to clarify that God is referring to all humanity and not simply the male sex when he says, "Let us make man in our image." Briefly answer any questions group members ask about any other words or phrases.

How the Bible Relates

1. In whose image were people made, according to the Bible? What do you think this means?

As you begin your discussion, clarify that the Bible assumes two things: (1) God exists, and (2) God created the universe and everything in it. Though your group members may not agree with these two points, ask them to set aside their questions for now and simply accept that these beliefs are basic to understanding the Bible.

The Bible says that something unique happened when God created human beings. **How did God distinguish between humans and other creatures? What did God give to humans that he gave to no other creature?** Two things should become clear: Humans were created to "rule . . . over all the earth," and they were created by God "in his own image." Both clearly distinguish between humans and any other living creature.

Look more closely at the phrase "in his image." **Which characteristics of God do you think he may have given humans? What qualities set us apart from other living creatures? Might these differences be present because humans have been made "in the image of God"?** Allow group members to think about these questions and to wrestle with how humans might reflect some of the qualities of God.

The Scriptures do not explain "in his image" more specifically here, though other places hint of its meaning. For now, it is sufficient to establish that human beings have a special place in creation because they reflect some part of God's nature that animals do not.

 You might explore this a bit more in the longer format: **What makes you different from an animal? What qualities do you possess that a dog or horse or cat does not? How are human relationships different from those among animals or between animals and humans?** These questions will help group members focus on those special qualities that God has given them.

You may want to look at one more aspect of the image of God: "male and female he created them." The preceding verse says "in the image of God he created him, male and female. . . ." **What does this suggest about God? Though we speak of God as "he" or "him," how might "male and female" reflect God's image and likeness?** Affirm that while God is a spirit and neither male nor female, the best qualities of both male and female originate in God, who created them both.

Members may ask about the word "our" in relationship to God ("in our image," "our likeness"). They might wonder if that means that there is more than one God. The Bible speaks of one true and living God, who has revealed himself in three persons: Father, Son, and Holy Spirit. This is a mystery of the Christian faith, something that no one can fully understand or explain, but which must simply be accepted in faith.

2. What was their job description?

This may be an eye-opener for some group members. **What role do human beings play, compared with all other creatures? How far does human rule extend? What do you think God means by "rule"?** Use these questions to help your members see that humans enjoy an almost godlike position on earth, with the job of overseeing all other creatures. But God's words indicate that he has in mind more of a caring servanthood than a tyranny that exploits the world for its own desires and whims.

 In the longer format, relate God's command to some of the situations we face. **How might this translate into some of today's environmental issues?** This should lead naturally into the next discussion question.

3. How might this perspective affect how we treat each other and our world?

You've already touched on how God has intended us to treat our world. Explore this in more detail, if you wish; but be sure also to deal with how God expects us to treat each other.

As you do so, consider the following questions: **What are some ways that our society views people? How can you "use" another person (or part of the earth's resources) for your own purposes? How does that happen in our society?** Your group should have a lot to talk about here. Many of the problems that our society faces today—rising crime, spouse and child abuse, teenage pregnancy, poverty issues—have their roots in how people see each other. If we see others only as means to an end or as objects that help us to achieve our own goals and desires, then we have lost a respect for each other's rights and dignity.

Without that respect, crime is easy. Studies show that the most hardened criminals are those who failed to bond with a parent or authority figure. They have never learned to love and respect another person.

But that's not all. Not only do we not respect others, but we also do not respect ourselves. Many people consider themselves useless, worthless, and hopeless. **How does that perspective affect a person's life? How does the Bible's account of our beginnings give us a different view of ourselves? What difference might that make to someone who suffers from a broken and hopeless view of his or her existence?**

How do you think God intended us to treat each other, in light of this passage? Use this question to affirm again the goodness in relationships—respect, love, and care—that comprise healthy relationships.

4. According to Romans, what do all people have in common?

At this point, your group will begin to deal with the question "What went wrong with God's good plan?" You might look first at the phrase "all have sinned." **What is** sin? **Is sin only great and terrible wrongs, or is it also small, everyday wrongs?** Sit back and listen to your group members talk about sin.

Many people today think that "sin" refers only to terrible atrocities—mass murders, Hitler-type violence, and so on. But the Bible looks at sin in a simpler, broader way. To Christians, sin means simply "missing the mark." In other words, it's failing to live how God intended us to live. **What does the Genesis passage tell us about how God intended us to live? How have we missed that mark?** Your discussion of broken relationships and a scarred creation should quickly point up the undeniable presence of sin in all of our lives. Be as specific as you can to help group members understand the power and impact of sin.

 In the longer format, briefly retell the story of Adam and Eve's disobedience in the Garden of Eden for group members who may be unfamiliar with it. Help them realize that humans were created perfect and splendid—and then, because of their own wrongdoing, became marred and stained with sin.

Because of sin, we all "fall short of the glory of God." **What is "glory"?** Webster describes the word "glory" as "praise, honor, or distinction . . . something that secures praise or renown . . . great beauty or splendor . . . something marked by beauty and resplendence." **What kind of glory were people created to have, according to Genesis 1? How have they fallen short of this?** These questions should merely reinforce what your group members have been discovering throughout this discussion: God created us to fulfill a splendid and beautiful role in his creation—and human society today certainly does not reflect what God had intended it to be.

Imagine what God's glory might be like. If you wish, read a few verses from the Psalms (e.g., Psalm 89:5-8; 96; 97:1-6) or from Isaiah 40 that describe God's glory and majesty. **How can someone who lies or cheats or steals or hurts others share in that glory?** As it stands, no one can. That's the bad news.

But the good news—that's what the word "gospel" means—is this: God offers to make everything right again. Let your group know that God has not left things to stand as they are, hopelessly mired in sin. The next session will deal with the good news of the gospel message. Whet group members' appetite for hearing that good news by referring to it briefly here.

 In the longer format, you will have time to explore this more fully, especially if you sense that some group members are ready to hear and respond to the good news of God's love and forgiveness in Jesus.

5. In your experience, does the Bible's teaching on human nature seem true? Why or why not?

Use this time to listen to what your group members have learned from this session. Don't give them the impression that you're looking for "right" answers here; encourage them to explore their own questions and struggles honestly. If some hold different views from those of Genesis and Romans, it may take a long time for them to change those basic and fundamental beliefs. Encourage them to explore the Bible's perspective honestly and thoroughly.

The Bottom Line

The Bible gives us good news and bad news. The good news is this: All people have been created in God's likeness, with a great potential for doing good on this earth. The bad news is that the image of God in us is completely tarnished because of sin. But more good news follows the bad: God offers us a way to get back all we've lost.

Read through the "Bottom Line" with your group and again affirm that God has offered each of us a way to regain all that we've lost: a restored friendship with God, healed relationships with each other, a rebuilding of God's qualities and character within us, and the ability to restore and work with God's creation.

Optional Prayer Time

Ask for needs for which group members would like prayer during the week. Follow up on earlier concerns and make a mental note of anything shared that may call for a card of encouragement, a phone call to say "How are you doing?" or a meal or other tangible expression of help during this week.

Prayer

Dear God, help me to take time in my busyness to think about where I came from and what you intend my life to be. Help me to honestly face areas of wrongdoing in my life and to look to you for help. Amen.

A Final Word

O Lord our God, the majesty and glory of your name fills all the earth and overflows the heavens. When I look up into the night skies and see the work of your fingers—the moon and stars you have made—I cannot understand how you can bother with mere puny man, to pay any attention to him! And yet you have made him only a little lower than the angels, and placed a crown of glory and honor upon his head. You have put him in charge of everything you made. *(David in Psalm 8:1, 3-6, The Living Bible)*

5: The Truth About Humanity

Beginnings

What is the best thing you can think of about being a man? A woman? What is the worst thing about it? We live on a planet with millions of other kinds of living creatures. Major differences separate humans and other living creatures. What are these differences?

What's Happening Today

This world teems with all kinds of living creatures. But one kind of inhabitant has affected the condition of this world more than any other: humans.

Where wilderness once stretched for thousands of miles, farmland and homes and factories and paved roads now cover the land. Rivers are dammed into reservoirs, trees are chopped down, deserts are irrigated, wild animals are driven back, rain forests are disappearing. Oceans are crisscrossed with freight ships, skies with airliners, and outer space with satellites and space shuttles.

No other creature has begun to affect this world as humans have. Amazing scientific discoveries and pioneering inventions reveal the creativity and intelligence of the human mind. Our plans and needs have dominated and shaped most of the inhabitable parts of the world.

We also communicate and relate to each other on a far different level than other living creatures do. Music, poetry, newspapers, computers, books and stories, television—all help us speak and hear each other's dreams, ideas, feelings, and needs.

Yet for all our achievements, stories of violence and suffering darken our newscasts night after night. Divorce, rape, murder, theft, dishonesty, child abuse, environmental abuse, pollution, cheating, hunger, poverty, drugs—these reveal the dark side of the human spirit.

Where does that dark side come from? Where do we come from? Did we evolve or were we created? What does it mean to be human? What are we supposed to be doing with the world we live in?

The Bible answers these questions and helps us understand ourselves. Look at these answers and see if they help you make sense out of your own life.

What the Bible Tells Us

Then God said, "Let us make man in our image, in our likeness, and let them rule over the fish of the sea and the birds of the air, over the livestock, over all the earth, and over all the creatures that move along the ground."

So God created man in his own image,
in the image of God he created him,
male and female he created them.

God blessed them and said to them, "Be fruitful and increase in number; fill the earth and subdue it. Rule over the fish of the sea and the birds of the air and over every living creature that moves on the ground." (Genesis 1:26-28)

There is no difference, for all have sinned and fall short of the glory of God. (Romans 3:23)

How the Bible Relates

1. In whose image were people made, according to the Bible? What do you think this means?

2. What was their job description?

3. How might this perspective affect how we treat each other and our world?

4. According to Romans, what do all people have in common?

5. In your experience, does the Bible's teaching on human nature seem true? Why or why not?

The Bottom Line

The Bible gives us good news and bad news. The good news is this: All people have been created in God's likeness, with a great potential for doing good on this earth. The bad news is that the image of God in us is completely tarnished because of sin. But more good news follows the bad: God offers us a way to get back all we've lost.

Prayer

Dear God, help me to take time in my busyness to think about where I came from and what you intend my life to be. Help me to honestly face areas of wrongdoing in my life and to look to you for help. Amen.

A Final Word

O Lord our God, the majesty and glory of your name fills all the earth and overflows the heavens. When I look up into the night skies and see the work of your fingers—the moon and stars you have made—I cannot understand how you can bother with mere puny man, to pay any attention to him! And yet you have made him only a little lower than the angels, and placed a crown of glory and honor upon his head. You have put him in charge of everything you made. *(David in Psalm 8:1, 3-6, The Living Bible)*

5: The Truth About Humanity

Beginnings

What is the best thing you can think of about being a man? A woman? What is the worst thing about it? We live on a planet with millions of other kinds of living creatures. Major differences separate humans and other living creatures. What are these differences?

What's Happening Today

This world teems with all kinds of living creatures. But one kind of inhabitant has affected the condition of this world more than any other: humans.

Where wilderness once stretched for thousands of miles, farmland and homes and factories and paved roads now cover the land. Rivers are dammed into reservoirs, trees are chopped down, deserts are irrigated, wild animals are driven back, rain forests are disappearing. Oceans are crisscrossed with freight ships, skies with airliners, and outer space with satellites and space shuttles.

No other creature has begun to affect this world as humans have. Amazing scientific discoveries and pioneering inventions reveal the creativity and intelligence of the human mind. Our plans and needs have dominated and shaped most of the inhabitable parts of the world.

We also communicate and relate to each other on a far different level than other living creatures do. Music, poetry, newspapers, computers, books and stories, television—all help us speak and hear each other's dreams, ideas, feelings, and needs.

Yet for all our achievements, stories of violence and suffering darken our newscasts night after night. Divorce, rape, murder, theft, dishonesty, child abuse, environmental abuse, pollution, cheating, hunger, poverty, drugs—these reveal the dark side of the human spirit.

Where does that dark side come from? Where do we come from? Did we evolve or were we created? What does it mean to be human? What are we supposed to be doing with the world we live in?

The Bible answers these questions and helps us understand ourselves. Look at these answers and see if they help you make sense out of your own life.

What the Bible Tells Us

Then God said, "Let us make man in our image, in our likeness, and let them rule over the fish of the sea and the birds of the air, over the livestock, over all the earth, and over all the creatures that move along the ground."

So God created man in his own image,
in the image of God he created him,
male and female he created them.

God blessed them and said to them, "Be fruitful and increase in number; fill the earth and subdue it. Rule over the fish of the sea and the birds of the air and over every living creature that moves on the ground." (Genesis 1:26-28)

There is no difference, for all have sinned and fall short of the glory of God. (Romans 3:23)

How the Bible Relates

1. In whose image were people made, according to the Bible? What do you think this means?

2. What was their job description?

3. How might this perspective affect how we treat each other and our world?

4. According to Romans, what do all people have in common?

5. In your experience, does the Bible's teaching on human nature seem true? Why or why not?

The Bottom Line

The Bible gives us good news and bad news. The good news is this: All people have been created in God's likeness, with a great potential for doing good on this earth. The bad news is that the image of God in us is completely tarnished because of sin. But more good news follows the bad: God offers us a way to get back all we've lost.

Prayer

Dear God, help me to take time in my busyness to think about where I came from and what you intend my life to be. Help me to honestly face areas of wrongdoing in my life and to look to you for help. Amen.

A Final Word

O Lord our God, the majesty and glory of your name fills all the earth and overflows the heavens. When I look up into the night skies and see the work of your fingers—the moon and stars you have made—I cannot understand how you can bother with mere puny man, to pay any attention to him! And yet you have made him only a little lower than the angels, and placed a crown of glory and honor upon his head. You have put him in charge of everything you made. *(David in Psalm 8:1, 3-6, The Living Bible)*

5: The Truth About Humanity

Beginnings

What is the best thing you can think of about being a man? A woman? What is the worst thing about it? We live on a planet with millions of other kinds of living creatures. Major differences separate humans and other living creatures. What are these differences?

What's Happening Today

This world teems with all kinds of living creatures. But one kind of inhabitant has affected the condition of this world more than any other: humans.

Where wilderness once stretched for thousands of miles, farmland and homes and factories and paved roads now cover the land. Rivers are dammed into reservoirs, trees are chopped down, deserts are irrigated, wild animals are driven back, rain forests are disappearing. Oceans are crisscrossed with freight ships, skies with airliners, and outer space with satellites and space shuttles.

No other creature has begun to affect this world as humans have. Amazing scientific discoveries and pioneering inventions reveal the creativity and intelligence of the human mind. Our plans and needs have dominated and shaped most of the inhabitable parts of the world.

We also communicate and relate to each other on a far different level than other living creatures do. Music, poetry, newspapers, computers, books and stories, television—all help us speak and hear each other's dreams, ideas, feelings, and needs.

Yet for all our achievements, stories of violence and suffering darken our newscasts night after night. Divorce, rape, murder, theft, dishonesty, child abuse, environmental abuse, pollution, cheating, hunger, poverty, drugs—these reveal the dark side of the human spirit.

Where does that dark side come from? Where do we come from? Did we evolve or were we created? What does it mean to be human? What are we supposed to be doing with the world we live in?

The Bible answers these questions and helps us understand ourselves. Look at these answers and see if they help you make sense out of your own life.

What the Bible Tells Us

Then God said, "Let us make man in our image, in our likeness, and let them rule over the fish of the sea and the birds of the air, over the livestock, over all the earth, and over all the creatures that move along the ground."

So God created man in his own image,
in the image of God he created him,
male and female he created them.

God blessed them and said to them, "Be fruitful and increase in number; fill the earth and subdue it. Rule over the fish of the sea and the birds of the air and over every living creature that moves on the ground." (Genesis 1:26-28)

There is no difference, for all have sinned and fall short of the glory of God. (Romans 3:23)

How the Bible Relates

1. In whose image were people made, according to the Bible? What do you think this means?

2. What was their job description?

3. How might this perspective affect how we treat each other and our world?

4. According to Romans, what do all people have in common?

5. In your experience, does the Bible's teaching on human nature seem true? Why or why not?

The Bottom Line

The Bible gives us good news and bad news. The good news is this: All people have been created in God's likeness, with a great potential for doing good on this earth. The bad news is that the image of God in us is completely tarnished because of sin. But more good news follows the bad: God offers us a way to get back all we've lost.

Prayer

Dear God, help me to take time in my busyness to think about where I came from and what you intend my life to be. Help me to honestly face areas of wrongdoing in my life and to look to you for help. Amen.

A Final Word

O Lord our God, the majesty and glory of your name fills all the earth and overflows the heavens. When I look up into the night skies and see the work of your fingers—the moon and stars you have made—I cannot understand how you can bother with mere puny man, to pay any attention to him! And yet you have made him only a little lower than the angels, and placed a crown of glory and honor upon his head. You have put him in charge of everything you made. *(David in Psalm 8:1, 3-6, The Living Bible)*

5: The Truth About Humanity

Beginnings

What is the best thing you can think of about being a man? A woman? What is the worst thing about it? We live on a planet with millions of other kinds of living creatures. Major differences separate humans and other living creatures. What are these differences?

What's Happening Today

This world teems with all kinds of living creatures. But one kind of inhabitant has affected the condition of this world more than any other: humans.

Where wilderness once stretched for thousands of miles, farmland and homes and factories and paved roads now cover the land. Rivers are dammed into reservoirs, trees are chopped down, deserts are irrigated, wild animals are driven back, rain forests are disappearing. Oceans are crisscrossed with freight ships, skies with airliners, and outer space with satellites and space shuttles.

No other creature has begun to affect this world as humans have. Amazing scientific discoveries and pioneering inventions reveal the creativity and intelligence of the human mind. Our plans and needs have dominated and shaped most of the inhabitable parts of the world.

We also communicate and relate to each other on a far different level than other living creatures do. Music, poetry, newspapers, computers, books and stories, television—all help us speak and hear each other's dreams, ideas, feelings, and needs.

Yet for all our achievements, stories of violence and suffering darken our newscasts night after night. Divorce, rape, murder, theft, dishonesty, child abuse, environmental abuse, pollution, cheating, hunger, poverty, drugs—these reveal the dark side of the human spirit.

Where does that dark side come from? Where do we come from? Did we evolve or were we created? What does it mean to be human? What are we supposed to be doing with the world we live in?

The Bible answers these questions and helps us understand ourselves. Look at these answers and see if they help you make sense out of your own life.

What the Bible Tells Us

Then God said, "Let us make man in our image, in our likeness, and let them rule over the fish of the sea and the birds of the air, over the livestock, over all the earth, and over all the creatures that move along the ground."

So God created man in his own image,
in the image of God he created him,
male and female he created them.

God blessed them and said to them, "Be fruitful and increase in number; fill the earth and subdue it. Rule over the fish of the sea and the birds of the air and over every living creature that moves on the ground." (Genesis 1:26-28)

There is no difference, for all have sinned and fall short of the glory of God. (Romans 3:23)

How the Bible Relates

1. In whose image were people made, according to the Bible? What do you think this means?

2. What was their job description?

3. How might this perspective affect how we treat each other and our world?

4. According to Romans, what do all people have in common?

5. In your experience, does the Bible's teaching on human nature seem true? Why or why not?

The Bottom Line

The Bible gives us good news and bad news. The good news is this: All people have been created in God's likeness, with a great potential for doing good on this earth. The bad news is that the image of God in us is completely tarnished because of sin. But more good news follows the bad: God offers us a way to get back all we've lost.

Prayer

Dear God, help me to take time in my busyness to think about where I came from and what you intend my life to be. Help me to honestly face areas of wrongdoing in my life and to look to you for help. Amen.

A Final Word

O Lord our God, the majesty and glory of your name fills all the earth and overflows the heavens. When I look up into the night skies and see the work of your fingers—the moon and stars you have made—I cannot understand how you can bother with mere puny man, to pay any attention to him! And yet you have made him only a little lower than the angels, and placed a crown of glory and honor upon his head. You have put him in charge of everything you made. *(David in Psalm 8:1, 3-6, The Living Bible)*

5: The Truth About Humanity

Beginnings

What is the best thing you can think of about being a man? A woman? What is the worst thing about it? We live on a planet with millions of other kinds of living creatures. Major differences separate humans and other living creatures. What are these differences?

What's Happening Today

This world teems with all kinds of living creatures. But one kind of inhabitant has affected the condition of this world more than any other: humans.

Where wilderness once stretched for thousands of miles, farmland and homes and factories and paved roads now cover the land. Rivers are dammed into reservoirs, trees are chopped down, deserts are irrigated, wild animals are driven back, rain forests are disappearing. Oceans are crisscrossed with freight ships, skies with airliners, and outer space with satellites and space shuttles.

No other creature has begun to affect this world as humans have. Amazing scientific discoveries and pioneering inventions reveal the creativity and intelligence of the human mind. Our plans and needs have dominated and shaped most of the inhabitable parts of the world.

We also communicate and relate to each other on a far different level than other living creatures do. Music, poetry, newspapers, computers, books and stories, television—all help us speak and hear each other's dreams, ideas, feelings, and needs.

Yet for all our achievements, stories of violence and suffering darken our newscasts night after night. Divorce, rape, murder, theft, dishonesty, child abuse, environmental abuse, pollution, cheating, hunger, poverty, drugs—these reveal the dark side of the human spirit.

Where does that dark side come from? Where do we come from? Did we evolve or were we created? What does it mean to be human? What are we supposed to be doing with the world we live in?

The Bible answers these questions and helps us understand ourselves. Look at these answers and see if they help you make sense out of your own life.

What the Bible Tells Us

Then God said, "Let us make man in our image, in our likeness, and let them rule over the fish of the sea and the birds of the air, over the livestock, over all the earth, and over all the creatures that move along the ground."

So God created man in his own image,
in the image of God he created him,
male and female he created them.

God blessed them and said to them, "Be fruitful and increase in number; fill the earth and subdue it. Rule over the fish of the sea and the birds of the air and over every living creature that moves on the ground." (Genesis 1:26-28)

There is no difference, for all have sinned and fall short of the glory of God. (Romans 3:23)

How the Bible Relates

1. In whose image were people made, according to the Bible? What do you think this means?

2. What was their job description?

3. How might this perspective affect how we treat each other and our world?

4. According to Romans, what do all people have in common?

5. In your experience, does the Bible's teaching on human nature seem true? Why or why not?

The Bottom Line

The Bible gives us good news and bad news. The good news is this: All people have been created in God's likeness, with a great potential for doing good on this earth. The bad news is that the image of God in us is completely tarnished because of sin. But more good news follows the bad: God offers us a way to get back all we've lost.

Prayer

Dear God, help me to take time in my busyness to think about where I came from and what you intend my life to be. Help me to honestly face areas of wrongdoing in my life and to look to you for help. Amen.

A Final Word

O Lord our God, the majesty and glory of your name fills all the earth and overflows the heavens. When I look up into the night skies and see the work of your fingers—the moon and stars you have made—I cannot understand how you can bother with mere puny man, to pay any attention to him! And yet you have made him only a little lower than the angels, and placed a crown of glory and honor upon his head. You have put him in charge of everything you made. *(David in Psalm 8:1, 3-6, The Living Bible)*

5: The Truth About Humanity

Beginnings

What is the best thing you can think of about being a man? A woman? What is the worst thing about it? We live on a planet with millions of other kinds of living creatures. Major differences separate humans and other living creatures. What are these differences?

What's Happening Today

This world teems with all kinds of living creatures. But one kind of inhabitant has affected the condition of this world more than any other: humans.

Where wilderness once stretched for thousands of miles, farmland and homes and factories and paved roads now cover the land. Rivers are dammed into reservoirs, trees are chopped down, deserts are irrigated, wild animals are driven back, rain forests are disappearing. Oceans are crisscrossed with freight ships, skies with airliners, and outer space with satellites and space shuttles.

No other creature has begun to affect this world as humans have. Amazing scientific discoveries and pioneering inventions reveal the creativity and intelligence of the human mind. Our plans and needs have dominated and shaped most of the inhabitable parts of the world.

We also communicate and relate to each other on a far different level than other living creatures do. Music, poetry, newspapers, computers, books and stories, television—all help us speak and hear each other's dreams, ideas, feelings, and needs.

Yet for all our achievements, stories of violence and suffering darken our newscasts night after night. Divorce, rape, murder, theft, dishonesty, child abuse, environmental abuse, pollution, cheating, hunger, poverty, drugs—these reveal the dark side of the human spirit.

Where does that dark side come from? Where do we come from? Did we evolve or were we created? What does it mean to be human? What are we supposed to be doing with the world we live in?

The Bible answers these questions and helps us understand ourselves. Look at these answers and see if they help you make sense out of your own life.

What the Bible Tells Us

Then God said, "Let us make man in our image, in our likeness, and let them rule over the fish of the sea and the birds of the air, over the livestock, over all the earth, and over all the creatures that move along the ground."

So God created man in his own image,
in the image of God he created him,
male and female he created them.

God blessed them and said to them, "Be fruitful and increase in number; fill the earth and subdue it. Rule over the fish of the sea and the birds of the air and over every living creature that moves on the ground." (Genesis 1:26-28)

There is no difference, for all have sinned and fall short of the glory of God. (Romans 3:23)

How the Bible Relates

1. In whose image were people made, according to the Bible? What do you think this means?

2. What was their job description?

3. How might this perspective affect how we treat each other and our world?

4. According to Romans, what do all people have in common?

5. In your experience, does the Bible's teaching on human nature seem true? Why or why not?

The Bottom Line

The Bible gives us good news and bad news. The good news is this: All people have been created in God's likeness, with a great potential for doing good on this earth. The bad news is that the image of God in us is completely tarnished because of sin. But more good news follows the bad: God offers us a way to get back all we've lost.

Prayer

Dear God, help me to take time in my busyness to think about where I came from and what you intend my life to be. Help me to honestly face areas of wrongdoing in my life and to look to you for help. Amen.

A Final Word

O Lord our God, the majesty and glory of your name fills all the earth and overflows the heavens. When I look up into the night skies and see the work of your fingers—the moon and stars you have made—I cannot understand how you can bother with mere puny man, to pay any attention to him! And yet you have made him only a little lower than the angels, and placed a crown of glory and honor upon his head. You have put him in charge of everything you made. *(David in Psalm 8:1, 3-6, The Living Bible)*

5: The Truth About Humanity

What is the best thing you can think of about being a man? A woman? What is the worst thing about it? We live on a planet with millions of other kinds of living creatures. Major differences separate humans and other living creatures. What are these differences?

What's Happening Today

This world teems with all kinds of living creatures. But one kind of inhabitant has affected the condition of this world more than any other: humans.

Where wilderness once stretched for thousands of miles, farmland and homes and factories and paved roads now cover the land. Rivers are dammed into reservoirs, trees are chopped down, deserts are irrigated, wild animals are driven back, rain forests are disappearing. Oceans are crisscrossed with freight ships, skies with airliners, and outer space with satellites and space shuttles.

No other creature has begun to affect this world as humans have. Amazing scientific discoveries and pioneering inventions reveal the creativity and intelligence of the human mind. Our plans and needs have dominated and shaped most of the inhabitable parts of the world.

We also communicate and relate to each other on a far different level than other living creatures do. Music, poetry, newspapers, computers, books and stories, television—all help us speak and hear each other's dreams, ideas, feelings, and needs.

Yet for all our achievements, stories of violence and suffering darken our newscasts night after night. Divorce, rape, murder, theft, dishonesty, child abuse, environmental abuse, pollution, cheating, hunger, poverty, drugs—these reveal the dark side of the human spirit.

Where does that dark side come from? Where do we come from? Did we evolve or were we created? What does it mean to be human? What are we supposed to be doing with the world we live in?

The Bible answers these questions and helps us understand ourselves. Look at these answers and see if they help you make sense out of your own life.

What the Bible Tells Us

Then God said, "Let us make man in our image, in our likeness, and let them rule over the fish of the sea and the birds of the air, over the livestock, over all the earth, and over all the creatures that move along the ground."

So God created man in his own image,
in the image of God he created him,
male and female he created them.

God blessed them and said to them, "Be fruitful and increase in number; fill the earth and subdue it. Rule over the fish of the sea and the birds of the air and over every living creature that moves on the ground." (Genesis 1:26-28)

There is no difference, for all have sinned and fall short of the glory of God. (Romans 3:23)

How the Bible Relates

1. In whose image were people made, according to the Bible? What do you think this means?

2. What was their job description?

3. How might this perspective affect how we treat each other and our world?

4. According to Romans, what do all people have in common?

5. In your experience, does the Bible's teaching on human nature seem true? Why or why not?

The Bottom Line

The Bible gives us good news and bad news. The good news is this: All people have been created in God's likeness, with a great potential for doing good on this earth. The bad news is that the image of God in us is completely tarnished because of sin. But more good news follows the bad: God offers us a way to get back all we've lost.

Prayer

Dear God, help me to take time in my busyness to think about where I came from and what you intend my life to be. Help me to honestly face areas of wrongdoing in my life and to look to you for help. Amen.

A Final Word

O Lord our God, the majesty and glory of your name fills all the earth and overflows the heavens. When I look up into the night skies and see the work of your fingers—the moon and stars you have made—I cannot understand how you can bother with mere puny man, to pay any attention to him! And yet you have made him only a little lower than the angels, and placed a crown of glory and honor upon his head. You have put him in charge of everything you made. *(David in Psalm 8:1, 3-6, The Living Bible)*

5: The Truth About Humanity

Beginnings

What is the best thing you can think of about being a man? A woman? What is the worst thing about it? We live on a planet with millions of other kinds of living creatures. Major differences separate humans and other living creatures. What are these differences?

What's Happening Today

This world teems with all kinds of living creatures. But one kind of inhabitant has affected the condition of this world more than any other: humans.

Where wilderness once stretched for thousands of miles, farmland and homes and factories and paved roads now cover the land. Rivers are dammed into reservoirs, trees are chopped down, deserts are irrigated, wild animals are driven back, rain forests are disappearing. Oceans are crisscrossed with freight ships, skies with airliners, and outer space with satellites and space shuttles.

No other creature has begun to affect this world as humans have. Amazing scientific discoveries and pioneering inventions reveal the creativity and intelligence of the human mind. Our plans and needs have dominated and shaped most of the inhabitable parts of the world.

We also communicate and relate to each other on a far different level than other living creatures do. Music, poetry, newspapers, computers, books and stories, television—all help us speak and hear each other's dreams, ideas, feelings, and needs.

Yet for all our achievements, stories of violence and suffering darken our newscasts night after night. Divorce, rape, murder, theft, dishonesty, child abuse, environmental abuse, pollution, cheating, hunger, poverty, drugs—these reveal the dark side of the human spirit.

Where does that dark side come from? Where do we come from? Did we evolve or were we created? What does it mean to be human? What are we supposed to be doing with the world we live in?

The Bible answers these questions and helps us understand ourselves. Look at these answers and see if they help you make sense out of your own life.

What the Bible Tells Us

Then God said, "Let us make man in our image, in our likeness, and let them rule over the fish of the sea and the birds of the air, over the livestock, over all the earth, and over all the creatures that move along the ground."

So God created man in his own image,
in the image of God he created him,
male and female he created them.

God blessed them and said to them, "Be fruitful and increase in number; fill the earth and subdue it. Rule over the fish of the sea and the birds of the air and over every living creature that moves on the ground." (Genesis 1:26-28)

There is no difference, for all have sinned and fall short of the glory of God. (Romans 3:23)

How the Bible Relates

1. In whose image were people made, according to the Bible? What do you think this means?

2. What was their job description?

3. How might this perspective affect how we treat each other and our world?

4. According to Romans, what do all people have in common?

5. In your experience, does the Bible's teaching on human nature seem true? Why or why not?

The Bible gives us good news and bad news. The good news is this: All people have been created in God's likeness, with a great potential for doing good on this earth. The bad news is that the image of God in us is completely tarnished because of sin. But more good news follows the bad: God offers us a way to get back all we've lost.

Prayer

Dear God, help me to take time in my busyness to think about where I came from and what you intend my life to be. Help me to honestly face areas of wrongdoing in my life and to look to you for help. Amen.

A Final Word

O Lord our God, the majesty and glory of your name fills all the earth and overflows the heavens. When I look up into the night skies and see the work of your fingers—the moon and stars you have made—I cannot understand how you can bother with mere puny man, to pay any attention to him! And yet you have made him only a little lower than the angels, and placed a crown of glory and honor upon his head. You have put him in charge of everything you made. *(David in Psalm 8:1, 3-6, The Living Bible)*

5: The Truth About Humanity

Beginnings

What is the best thing you can think of about being a man? A woman? What is the worst thing about it? We live on a planet with millions of other kinds of living creatures. Major differences separate humans and other living creatures. What are these differences?

What's Happening Today

This world teems with all kinds of living creatures. But one kind of inhabitant has affected the condition of this world more than any other: humans.

Where wilderness once stretched for thousands of miles, farmland and homes and factories and paved roads now cover the land. Rivers are dammed into reservoirs, trees are chopped down, deserts are irrigated, wild animals are driven back, rain forests are disappearing. Oceans are crisscrossed with freight ships, skies with airliners, and outer space with satellites and space shuttles.

No other creature has begun to affect this world as humans have. Amazing scientific discoveries and pioneering inventions reveal the creativity and intelligence of the human mind. Our plans and needs have dominated and shaped most of the inhabitable parts of the world.

We also communicate and relate to each other on a far different level than other living creatures do. Music, poetry, newspapers, computers, books and stories, television—all help us speak and hear each other's dreams, ideas, feelings, and needs.

Yet for all our achievements, stories of violence and suffering darken our newscasts night after night. Divorce, rape, murder, theft, dishonesty, child abuse, environmental abuse, pollution, cheating, hunger, poverty, drugs—these reveal the dark side of the human spirit.

Where does that dark side come from? Where do we come from? Did we evolve or were we created? What does it mean to be human? What are we supposed to be doing with the world we live in?

The Bible answers these questions and helps us understand ourselves. Look at these answers and see if they help you make sense out of your own life.

What the Bible Tells Us

Then God said, "Let us make man in our image, in our likeness, and let them rule over the fish of the sea and the birds of the air, over the livestock, over all the earth, and over all the creatures that move along the ground."

*So God created man in his own image,
in the image of God he created him,
male and female he created them.*

God blessed them and said to them, "Be fruitful and increase in number; fill the earth and subdue it. Rule over the fish of the sea and the birds of the air and over every living creature that moves on the ground." (Genesis 1:26-28)

There is no difference, for all have sinned and fall short of the glory of God. (Romans 3:23)

How the Bible Relates

1. In whose image were people made, according to the Bible? What do you think this means?

2. What was their job description?

3. How might this perspective affect how we treat each other and our world?

4. According to Romans, what do all people have in common?

5. In your experience, does the Bible's teaching on human nature seem true? Why or why not?

The Bottom Line

The Bible gives us good news and bad news. The good news is this: All people have been created in God's likeness, with a great potential for doing good on this earth. The bad news is that the image of God in us is completely tarnished because of sin. But more good news follows the bad: God offers us a way to get back all we've lost.

Prayer

Dear God, help me to take time in my busyness to think about where I came from and what you intend my life to be. Help me to honestly face areas of wrongdoing in my life and to look to you for help. Amen.

A Final Word

O Lord our God, the majesty and glory of your name fills all the earth and overflows the heavens. When I look up into the night skies and see the work of your fingers—the moon and stars you have made—I cannot understand how you can bother with mere puny man, to pay any attention to him! And yet you have made him only a little lower than the angels, and placed a crown of glory and honor upon his head. You have put him in charge of everything you made. *(David in Psalm 8:1, 3-6, The Living Bible)*

5: The Truth About Humanity

Beginnings

What is the best thing you can think of about being a man? A woman? What is the worst thing about it? We live on a planet with millions of other kinds of living creatures. Major differences separate humans and other living creatures. What are these differences?

What's Happening Today

This world teems with all kinds of living creatures. But one kind of inhabitant has affected the condition of this world more than any other: humans.

Where wilderness once stretched for thousands of miles, farmland and homes and factories and paved roads now cover the land. Rivers are dammed into reservoirs, trees are chopped down, deserts are irrigated, wild animals are driven back, rain forests are disappearing. Oceans are crisscrossed with freight ships, skies with airliners, and outer space with satellites and space shuttles.

No other creature has begun to affect this world as humans have. Amazing scientific discoveries and pioneering inventions reveal the creativity and intelligence of the human mind. Our plans and needs have dominated and shaped most of the inhabitable parts of the world.

We also communicate and relate to each other on a far different level than other living creatures do. Music, poetry, newspapers, computers, books and stories, television—all help us speak and hear each other's dreams, ideas, feelings, and needs.

Yet for all our achievements, stories of violence and suffering darken our newscasts night after night. Divorce, rape, murder, theft, dishonesty, child abuse, environmental abuse, pollution, cheating, hunger, poverty, drugs—these reveal the dark side of the human spirit.

Where does that dark side come from? Where do we come from? Did we evolve or were we created? What does it mean to be human? What are we supposed to be doing with the world we live in?

The Bible answers these questions and helps us understand ourselves. Look at these answers and see if they help you make sense out of your own life.

What the Bible Tells Us

Then God said, "Let us make man in our image, in our likeness, and let them rule over the fish of the sea and the birds of the air, over the livestock, over all the earth, and over all the creatures that move along the ground."

So God created man in his own image, in the image of God he created him, male and female he created them.

God blessed them and said to them, "Be fruitful and increase in number; fill the earth and subdue it. Rule over the fish of the sea and the birds of the air and over every living creature that moves on the ground." (Genesis 1:26-28)

There is no difference, for all have sinned and fall short of the glory of God. (Romans 3:23)

How the Bible Relates

1. In whose image were people made, according to the Bible? What do you think this means?

2. What was their job description?

3. How might this perspective affect how we treat each other and our world?

4. According to Romans, what do all people have in common?

5. In your experience, does the Bible's teaching on human nature seem true? Why or why not?

The Bottom Line

The Bible gives us good news and bad news. The good news is this: All people have been created in God's likeness, with a great potential for doing good on this earth. The bad news is that the image of God in us is completely tarnished because of sin. But more good news follows the bad: God offers us a way to get back all we've lost.

Prayer

Dear God, help me to take time in my busyness to think about where I came from and what you intend my life to be. Help me to honestly face areas of wrongdoing in my life and to look to you for help. Amen.

A Final Word

O Lord our God, the majesty and glory of your name fills all the earth and overflows the heavens. When I look up into the night skies and see the work of your fingers—the moon and stars you have made—I cannot understand how you can bother with mere puny man, to pay any attention to him! And yet you have made him only a little lower than the angels, and placed a crown of glory and honor upon his head. You have put him in charge of everything you made. *(David in Psalm 8:1, 3-6, The Living Bible)*

The Whole Truth and Nothing But the Truth

6: The Truth About Christianity

Introductory Notes

The primary focus of this session is the truth that Christianity is a unique religion. The person and work of Jesus make it unique. In his book *Why Should Anyone Believe Anything at All?* James Sire lists the following good reasons for believing the Christian faith:

— Jesus himself: his character of wisdom and compassion, the method and content of his teaching, his resurrection

— the historical reliability of the gospels

— the internal consistency and coherence of the Christian worldview and its power to provide the best explanation of life's tough issues

— the testimony of individual Christians and of countless Christian communities that down through the ages exhibit the transforming power of God in and among his faithful believers

Sire goes on to say that Jesus is the main reason for believing in Christianity. If any of your group members want to pursue the truth of Christianity, suggest that they read one of the gospels (starting with John's gospel), and experience new life in Christ.

This session will attempt to show the truth of the Christian faith by emphasizing the unique feature of Christianity—salvation by grace alone. All other religions promote living a life that will appease a higher power. Christianity is the only religion based not on good works, but on God's redemptive grace in Christ Jesus.

This session will concentrate on the core gospel message. Keep in mind that Christians are often considered narrow-minded and too exclusive when they state that Christianity is the only way to become right with God. Our society prefers to allow each person the "right" to his or her private beliefs, without others' affirmation or condemnation.

Gently but clearly state that two opposing beliefs cannot be true at the same time. For example, if Jesus is who he claims to be, Mohammed cannot be who he claimed to be. If Jesus claims to be the Alpha and Omega, the beginning and the end, Mohammed cannot also be the last and greatest prophet.

Use this session to present salvation as the wonderful, free gift from a loving heavenly Father. Don't be surprised if some in your group disagree. Allow the Holy Spirit to work. If they have questions, offer to talk with them after the session. If they ask a question that you cannot answer, tell them that you will look it up. Don't belittle other religions; simply present the message of the cross in a positive affirming way.

Note that outward obedience to a code of ethical behavior is strong in most religions. Generally speaking, followers of non-Christian religions outwardly behave no better or worse than followers of Christ. Thanks to common grace, millions of non-Christians are genuinely loving and caring individuals. They make excellent friends and neighbors. But despite appearances, they still need to trust in Christ alone for their ultimate salvation.

Remember that you do not stand alone in proclaiming Christ as the only way to God. Jesus proclaimed this too!

Beginning the Session

Warmly greet your group members as they arrive for today's session. People enjoy a friendly handshake and a smile. Be sure that any newcomers to your group feel welcomed too. Informally introduce any new group members, and ask everyone to give their names. Distribute the discussion handouts and make sure that everyone is seated comfortably.

Over the past several weeks you will have established a closer friendship with many of your group members. Some will trust you more than they did at the beginning of these sessions. Perhaps they will have concluded that you are a person they could confide in. This is the Spirit working in their lives. While you may be tempted to take the credit for yourself, praise God for these developing relationships.

Give your group members even more reasons to trust your integrity and faith. Let them know that you have been praying for them (and make sure you have). Tell them that their concerns are very important to you and to God. That is why you take the time to bring their requests to God in prayer during the week. Assure them that your interest in them as individuals will not end with this session.

Offer a brief prayer as you begin this session. Thank God for each person present and for the answers to prayer that God has already provided.

 In the longer session, invite your group members to tell how God has worked in their lives as a result of these discussion groups. Be sensitive to those who may yet feel uncomfortable sharing; don't push. But welcome stories from group members who are freer to speak out. **What changes have you experienced in your circumstances or situation in the past few weeks? Do you think these changes come from God? Why? What lessons have you learned from them? What new insights have you gained from our discussions of the last five sessions?**

Beginnings

What religious beliefs are you are familiar with? Share, if possible, a meaningful religious experience you had as a child. How do you deal with somebody whose religious views differ from yours?

If you do not already know the religious background of your group members, the "Beginnings" questions should bring out that information. Remember, at this point and throughout the lesson, never to belittle another person's religious convictions. Whatever you say about these religions should be said kindly and gently but with conviction.

 In the longer session, you might want to ask some of the following questions: **What difficulties might arise when parents hold differing religious views? What if one spouse follows a different religion? If you have children, do you believe you should encourage your children to have some kind of faith experience? Why?** Members of the same family often hold differing religious views. Don't be judgmental as you encourage your group members with these questions. Take a compassionate attitude for families that practice more than one religion. Those families often experience disharmony.

What's Happening Today

Many television commercials and network programming include or cover non-Christian religions. Even breath mints are advertised within the context of Eastern mysticism. Television and films promote the Hindu notion of reincarnation. Spouses, for instance, return not only in the form of ghosts but even of animals.

Have someone in your group read through this section, then briefly discuss what was read. Discuss the cultural context of this session, but do not be concerned if some in your group continue to believe that all religions are equally true. Refer back to session 3, "The Truth About Truth." Remind your group that some important elements of the Christian religion are not found in any other religion. Ask them to keep an open mind about this question and to consider the verses found in "What the Bible Tells Us."

What the Bible Tells Us

Read through the Scripture passages aloud, doing so slowly enough and with enough emphasis so that group members can catch the message clearly. If there are questions on any of the terms used, be sure to take the time to answer them before getting into the discussion questions.

How the Bible Relates

1. What did Christ do for us? What is unusual about that?

As you discuss the Scripture passages with your group, the essence of the gospel message should become apparent. Be sure to explain (in common terms) the meaning of sin, grace, and God's mercy. Some members of your group may not have a foundation in the Christian religion and these concepts will be new to them.

The following definitions may help:

sin—disobedience to God's will as he reveals it in human conscience and in his Word, the Bible. Sin has such a grip on humankind, the Bible teaches, that all people are sinners, even from before birth.

grace—undeserved favor from God, attained through Jesus Christ's death on the cross. Can be explained as God's Riches At Christ's Expense.

mercy—God's free and undeserved compassion.

Remember that it is the Holy Spirit who will open the eyes of your group. You are doing your part if you ask and answer questions with gentleness and respect.

Most people can acknowledge that the man Jesus died at some point in history. The story of a good man giving his life for unjust reasons is one that many can admire. The difficulty surfaces when individuals are faced with what Jesus' death means for them personally. His death was necessary because of their sin. The words of the hymn, "O Sacred Head, Now Wounded" are foreign to their thinking:

> My Lord, what you did suffer was all for sinners' gain;
> Mine, mine was the transgression, but yours the deadly pain.
> So here I kneel, my Savior, for I deserve your place;
> Look on me with your favor and save me by your grace.

Christ's death for sinful humans is not a reasonable, logical action from a human point of view. **What seem to be the motives behind Christ's death? What did God have to gain from this? What do we have to gain?** Use these questions to help group members wrestle with the immense depth of God's love for them revealed in these verses. Christ's death was God's provision of escape from the penalty of sin which all people deserve. In redeeming his sons and daughters, God has gained a renewed fellowship with his people who someday will enjoy eternity in God's presence. Believers also gained freedom from enslavement to sin and a bright future of fellowship with God.

2. According to Romans 5, what is God's attitude toward us?

You've already touched on God's attitude toward sinful people in your discussion of the unusual nature of Christ's death. God's attitude not only deals with his love, however, but also with his view of humankind. To him, all human beings are "still sinners."

Many people resist owning up to their sinfulness. Some of your group members may claim that because they are not as bad as other people—such as murderers, thieves, and rapists—they are not sinful. Instead, you may want to use the term "imperfect." Most people will agree that they are not perfect. Emphasize that Christ's purpose in coming was to die for humankind. You might say that it was a rescue mission to turn people away from the bad choices that were leading them away from God.

 In the expanded format, note that throughout history God has provided the opportunity for people to come back to him. Jesus appears on the scene in the first century only after countless Old Testament prophets had failed to provide a lasting relationship.

The good news is that despite humankind's complete immersion in sin, God repeatedly offers redemption to those who will believe. He has done this throughout history. He does this for us today in Christ. Why does God bother? The only answer is his great mercy and love.

3. When you think of the word "sinner," what comes to mind?

If the problem of sin has not come up in previous sessions, use this question to see what your group members think. Point out that the biblical view of sin often means "missing the mark" or "falling short." **Of what do we fall short? To what or whom do you think God compares us?** The measure of our sin is never a matter of comparing ourselves to other people; rather, we are required to compare ourselves to the standards set by a holy and righteous God.

Does sin involve only actions, things we do wrong? What else might be included? Jesus considered sin not only in the context of our actions but also in our thoughts and attitudes. He pointed out that lust, for example, is the same as adultery; hate carries the same consequences as murder. This may surprise your group members. Some may feel that God is being unfair by exacting the same penalty for our thought life as for our outward actions.

 In the expanded format, pursue this matter with your group. **Is God being unfair or overly strict by suggesting our thoughts or attitudes are sinful? Can we more easily control our outward actions than our thought life? Why or why not? How do our thoughts control or influence our actions? In what way are our actions a mirror image of our thoughts?** As you discuss these questions, be sure that your group understands that you did not invent this teaching; it is God's truth. Group members may disagree with what the Bible teaches concerning the nature and pervasiveness of sin, but their argument is not with you. It is with God.

4. How much can we do to change our spiritual condition? Who has done the work for us?

For some in your group, these questions may bring a new revelation: We can do nothing to become right with God. Perhaps these group members may have even come from a Christian background, but one that taught works over grace. If this is the case, clearly emphasize the biblical message of grace rather than works. Works do not achieve salvation for us. **If Jesus saves us by grace, not by what we do, why should we bother to do good works?** In the biblical scheme, works flow from gratitude for God's grace. Use a human example here. **If someone rescued you from a burning building and saved your life, what would you *want* to do to show your gratitude? Would having been saved from certain death suggest that you had "earned" the right to be saved by your rescuer?** The answer is obvious. The deed was done; the rescue completed. To think we can earn something *after the fact* is ridiculous. The same is true for Christ's saving us while we were helpless to help ourselves. The apostle Paul describes us in that condition as "dead in our . . . sins" (Ephesians 2:1).

For others in your group, this teaching will provide a tremendous sense of relief. **Why might knowing that we are saved by what Jesus did, not by what we must do, be a relief for people?** It's a comforting relief because they know instinctively that they are completely unable to make things right with God. **Why might it be difficult for us to admit we cannot please God or earn our way into heaven?** The reason may be a strong work ethic, but most likely it is a desire to control our own lives, a rebellious refusal to give God control. Some may find it difficult to admit that they can do nothing to please God. Others might feel that they don't owe God anything. That, too, comes from a desire to be the "masters of our fate, the captains of our soul."

Be sensitive to the internal conflicts that some group members may be experiencing. They are learning truths that you may have known and understood for many years. The discussion has dealt with the most important issues of life. Be patient and loving with strugglers as you encourage them to verbalize their thoughts and questions. If some in your group are not ready to receive the message of God's love and mercy, pray that God will open their eyes. Then continue to love them.

Press on gently to clarify some of the terms used in the Ephesians passage using the following questions. **What does the word "grace" mean to you? What example of a gracious act or a gracious person comes to mind? How might a parent show grace to a child? How might a judge show grace to a repentant prisoner? What good things can come from grace? What would you rather receive from God—grace or justice?** It may help to describe grace as God's undeserved favor toward us. A familiar acronym is this: God's Riches At Christ's Expense.

5. How does Christianity differ from what other religions teach about getting right with God?

The Ephesians passage teaches humankind's inability to make things right with God. This is one key place where Christianity and other religions radically differ. Every other belief system requires people to *do* something to please God. Christianity offers a better way. It acknowledges that people are unable to work their way into heaven. Instead, it offers Christ's free gift of forgiveness and salvation.

These verses from Romans and Ephesians have provided an opportunity to clearly present God's offer of salvation in Christ. Be sensitive to the Holy Spirit's guidance as you give the gospel invitation. If most members are still resistant or questioning, it may be best simply to invite those who have more questions on the Christian faith to meet with you afterward to talk and pray together. If your group seems very receptive to the message of the gospel, by all means offer to pray with them in your closing prayer time to accept the gift of God's love and forgiveness in Jesus.

The Bottom Line

The central message of Christianity is this: Jesus died so that imperfect people can have a saving relationship with a perfectly holy God. Furthermore, his resurrection proves that he was unique enough to accomplish this deed.

The death of an ordinary man, no matter how special, can do nothing more than inspire people. But if Jesus is who he claims to be, his resurrection confirms that his death was more than simply commitment to principle.

Most people are familiar with the lyrics of the hymn "Amazing Grace":

> Amazing grace, how sweet the sound
>   that saved a wretch like me.
> I once was lost, but now am found,
>   was blind, but now I see.

You might use these words of this hymn to review the key points of this session.

 In the longer session, offer your group members the time they need to ask questions, talk, and pray about God's offer through Jesus. You may find the following script helpful as you lead them through this discussion and prayer:

Listen now to what God is saying to you.

You may be aware of things in your life that keep you from coming near to God. You may have thought of God as someone who is unsympathetic, angry, and punishing. You may feel like you don't know how to pray to God or how to approach him.

Listen to what God is saying to you through Jesus. He is an understanding, loving God. He knows firsthand what it's like to live in a sinful, broken world. He knows how hard it is to overcome the constant temptation to sin. He has already taken the punishment for your sin, clearing the way for you to come near to God.

So now come near to God. It's as simple as A-B-C:

A dmit that you have sinned, and that you need God's forgiveness.

B elieve that God loves you and that Jesus has already paid the price for your sins.

C ommit your life to God in prayer, asking him to forgive your sins, make you his child, and fill you with his Holy Spirit.

Prayer of Commitment

This prayer can help you draw near to God:

Dear God, I believe that you love me. Please forgive me for all the things in my life that stand between you and me. Thank you for giving your only Son, Jesus, to die for my sins.

Now help me to believe in Jesus with all my heart. Help me to really accept that you came into the world to save me, not to condemn me. I believe that my sins are completely forgiven because of what Jesus did for me. Help me to remember that what I did in the past no longer makes me feel guilty or unworthy of being your child.

Thank you that you are making me completely new, that you will teach me through the Bible how to be your child. Give me your Holy Spirit now, to help me pray and to teach me from your Word.

In Jesus' name, amen.

Do not pressure anyone to respond at this point; remember that they may need time to think, reflect, and pray about God's offer to them. They may need to hear it again from you in a personal conversation or further Bible study. But let them know that God's offer is real and that they have a real hope for change and renewal in their lives.

When you have discussed any questions that group members may have, let them know that you are available after the study or during the coming weeks to talk with them further about God's offer in Christ. Make sure they have your phone number and know what hours they can reach you.

Encourage them as warmly as you can to contact you with any questions.

Prayer

God, if Christianity is truly unique, help me to see it and believe the truth. Amen.

Use your prayer time to pray—gently but with conviction—for the members of your group. Ask that God will help them to see the depth of love that he holds for them and the personal response that he desires from them. Ask especially that they will not turn away from the amazing grace that Jesus' death offers them.

A Final Word

Here is a trustworthy saying that deserves acceptance: Christ came into the world to save sinners. *(The apostle Paul in 1 Timothy 1:15)*

6: The Truth About Christianity

Beginnings

What religious beliefs are you familiar with? Share, if possible, a meaningful religious experience you had as a child. How do you deal with somebody whose religious views differ from yours?

What's Happening Today

North America is a pluralistic culture that includes people from many ethnic and religious backgrounds. As a result, most people have been exposed to people who do not share their religious beliefs.

Certainly the emergence of Islamic fundamentalism on the world scene has made us increasingly aware of that rapidly growing Eastern religion. Adherents of Islam appear on the evening news programs. Millions of faithful Muslims bow toward Mecca several times a day.

Eastern mysticism is becoming popular in Western society, fueled in part by Hollywood stars promoting the mystery of reincarnation. In addition, Eastern meditation has become a regular part of some people's daily routine.

Many of the world's religions have much in common. For example, Christianity, Judaism, Islam, and Mormonism all use sacred writings as part of their religious tradition. Religious figures have played a major part in Buddhism, Islam, Judaism, and Christianity. Most major religious groups have similar codes of conduct, including their own version of the Golden Rule.

For this reason, many people think that all religions worship the same God, although the religions may use different names for God. Some people think that the basic beliefs of all religions are essentially the same.

This is an interesting theory, but a close examination of the world's major religions reveals many essential differences. For example, each religion insists that it is the only reliable way to God.

Christianity is no exception. In session 3 we looked at some of the exclusive claims Jesus made about himself. The purpose of this session is not to discuss and compare each major religion, but to explain the unique beliefs of Christianity.

After discussing these beliefs, you may want to compare them with other major religions.

The only way to determine whether something is true is to look at the evidence. The facts about Christianity are found in the Bible. The following verses for today express the core of the Christian belief and explain what makes Christianity unique among all other religions.

What the Bible Tells Us

Christ died for us while we were still weak. We were living against God, but at the right time, Christ died for us. Very few people will die to save the life of someone else. Although perhaps for a good man someone might possibly die. But Christ died for us while we were still sinners. In this way God shows his great love for us. (Romans 5:6-8, New Century Version)

God's mercy is great, and he loved us very much. We were spiritually dead because of the things we did wrong against God. But God gave us new life with Christ. You have been saved by God's grace. . . . I mean that you are saved by grace, and you got that grace by believing. You did not save yourselves. It was a gift from God. You cannot brag that you are saved by the work you have done. (Ephesians 2:4-5, 8-9, New Century Version)

How the Bible Relates

1. What did Christ do for us? What is unusual about that?

2. According to Romans 5, what is God's attitude toward us?

3. When you think of the word "sinner," what comes to mind?

4. How much can we do to change our spiritual condition? Who has done the work for us?

5. How does Christianity differ from what other religions teach about getting right with God?

The Bottom Line

The central message of Christianity is this: Jesus died so that imperfect people can have a saving relationship with a perfectly holy God. Furthermore, his resurrection proves that he was unique enough to accomplish this deed.

Prayer

God, if Christianity is truly unique, help me to see it and believe the truth. Amen.

A Final Word

Here is a trustworthy saying that deserves acceptance: Christ came into the world to save sinners. *(The apostle Paul in 1 Timothy 1:15)*

6: The Truth About Christianity

Beginnings

What religious beliefs are you familiar with? Share, if possible, a meaningful religious experience you had as a child. How do you deal with somebody whose religious views differ from yours?

What's Happening Today

North America is a pluralistic culture that includes people from many ethnic and religious backgrounds. As a result, most people have been exposed to people who do not share their religious beliefs.

Certainly the emergence of Islamic fundamentalism on the world scene has made us increasingly aware of that rapidly growing Eastern religion. Adherents of Islam appear on the evening news programs. Millions of faithful Muslims bow toward Mecca several times a day.

Eastern mysticism is becoming popular in Western society, fueled in part by Hollywood stars promoting the mystery of reincarnation. In addition, Eastern meditation has become a regular part of some people's daily routine.

Many of the world's religions have much in common. For example, Christianity, Judaism, Islam, and Mormonism all use sacred writings as part of their religious tradition. Religious figures have played a major part in Buddhism, Islam, Judaism, and Christianity. Most major religious groups have similar codes of conduct, including their own version of the Golden Rule.

For this reason, many people think that all religions worship the same God, although the religions may use different names for God. Some people think that the basic beliefs of all religions are essentially the same.

This is an interesting theory, but a close examination of the world's major religions reveals many essential differences. For example, each religion insists that it is the only reliable way to God.

Christianity is no exception. In session 3 we looked at some of the exclusive claims Jesus made about himself. The purpose of this session is not to discuss and compare each major religion, but to explain the unique beliefs of Christianity.

After discussing these beliefs, you may want to compare them with other major religions.

The only way to determine whether something is true is to look at the evidence. The facts about Christianity are found in the Bible. The following verses for today express the core of the Christian belief and explain what makes Christianity unique among all other religions.

What the Bible Tells Us

Christ died for us while we were still weak. We were living against God, but at the right time, Christ died for us. Very few people will die to save the life of someone else. Although perhaps for a good man someone might possibly die. But Christ died for us while we were still sinners. In this way God shows his great love for us. (Romans 5:6-8, New Century Version)

God's mercy is great, and he loved us very much. We were spiritually dead because of the things we did wrong against God. But God gave us new life with Christ. You have been saved by God's grace. . . . I mean that you are saved by grace, and you got that grace by believing. You did not save yourselves. It was a gift from God. You cannot brag that you are saved by the work you have done. (Ephesians 2:4-5, 8-9, New Century Version)

How the Bible Relates

1. What did Christ do for us? What is unusual about that?

2. According to Romans 5, what is God's attitude toward us?

3. When you think of the word "sinner," what comes to mind?

4. How much can we do to change our spiritual condition? Who has done the work for us?

5. How does Christianity differ from what other religions teach about getting right with God?

The Bottom Line

The central message of Christianity is this: Jesus died so that imperfect people can have a saving relationship with a perfectly holy God. Furthermore, his resurrection proves that he was unique enough to accomplish this deed.

Prayer

God, if Christianity is truly unique, help me to see it and believe the truth. Amen.

A Final Word

Here is a trustworthy saying that deserves acceptance: Christ came into the world to save sinners. *(The apostle Paul in 1 Timothy 1:15)*

6: The Truth About Christianity

Beginnings

What religious beliefs are you familiar with? Share, if possible, a meaningful religious experience you had as a child. How do you deal with somebody whose religious views differ from yours?

What's Happening Today

North America is a pluralistic culture that includes people from many ethnic and religious backgrounds. As a result, most people have been exposed to people who do not share their religious beliefs.

Certainly the emergence of Islamic fundamentalism on the world scene has made us increasingly aware of that rapidly growing Eastern religion. Adherents of Islam appear on the evening news programs. Millions of faithful Muslims bow toward Mecca several times a day.

Eastern mysticism is becoming popular in Western society, fueled in part by Hollywood stars promoting the mystery of reincarnation. In addition, Eastern meditation has become a regular part of some people's daily routine.

Many of the world's religions have much in common. For example, Christianity, Judaism, Islam, and Mormonism all use sacred writings as part of their religious tradition. Religious figures have played a major part in Buddhism, Islam, Judaism, and Christianity. Most major religious groups have similar codes of conduct, including their own version of the Golden Rule.

For this reason, many people think that all religions worship the same God, although the religions may use different names for God. Some people think that the basic beliefs of all religions are essentially the same.

This is an interesting theory, but a close examination of the world's major religions reveals many essential differences. For example, each religion insists that it is the only reliable way to God.

Christianity is no exception. In session 3 we looked at some of the exclusive claims Jesus made about himself. The purpose of this session is not to discuss and compare each major religion, but to explain the unique beliefs of Christianity.

After discussing these beliefs, you may want to compare them with other major religions.

The only way to determine whether something is true is to look at the evidence. The facts about Christianity are found in the Bible. The following verses for today express the core of the Christian belief and explain what makes Christianity unique among all other religions.

What the Bible Tells Us

Christ died for us while we were still weak. We were living against God, but at the right time, Christ died for us. Very few people will die to save the life of someone else. Although perhaps for a good man someone might possibly die. But Christ died for us while we were still sinners. In this way God shows his great love for us. (Romans 5:6-8, New Century Version)

God's mercy is great, and he loved us very much. We were spiritually dead because of the things we did wrong against God. But God gave us new life with Christ. You have been saved by God's grace. . . . I mean that you are saved by grace, and you got that grace by believing. You did not save yourselves. It was a gift from God. You cannot brag that you are saved by the work you have done. (Ephesians 2:4-5, 8-9, New Century Version)

How the Bible Relates

1. What did Christ do for us? What is unusual about that?

2. According to Romans 5, what is God's attitude toward us?

3. When you think of the word "sinner," what comes to mind?

4. How much can we do to change our spiritual condition? Who has done the work for us?

5. How does Christianity differ from what other religions teach about getting right with God?

The Bottom Line

The central message of Christianity is this: Jesus died so that imperfect people can have a saving relationship with a perfectly holy God. Furthermore, his resurrection proves that he was unique enough to accomplish this deed.

Prayer

God, if Christianity is truly unique, help me to see it and believe the truth. Amen.

A Final Word

Here is a trustworthy saying that deserves acceptance: Christ came into the world to save sinners. *(The apostle Paul in 1 Timothy 1:15)*

6: The Truth About Christianity

Beginnings

What religious beliefs are you familiar with? Share, if possible, a meaningful religious experience you had as a child. How do you deal with somebody whose religious views differ from yours?

What's Happening Today

North America is a pluralistic culture that includes people from many ethnic and religious backgrounds. As a result, most people have been exposed to people who do not share their religious beliefs.

Certainly the emergence of Islamic fundamentalism on the world scene has made us increasingly aware of that rapidly growing Eastern religion. Adherents of Islam appear on the evening news programs. Millions of faithful Muslims bow toward Mecca several times a day.

Eastern mysticism is becoming popular in Western society, fueled in part by Hollywood stars promoting the mystery of reincarnation. In addition, Eastern meditation has become a regular part of some people's daily routine.

Many of the world's religions have much in common. For example, Christianity, Judaism, Islam, and Mormonism all use sacred writings as part of their religious tradition. Religious figures have played a major part in Buddhism, Islam, Judaism, and Christianity. Most major religious groups have similar codes of conduct, including their own version of the Golden Rule.

For this reason, many people think that all religions worship the same God, although the religions may use different names for God. Some people think that the basic beliefs of all religions are essentially the same.

This is an interesting theory, but a close examination of the world's major religions reveals many essential differences. For example, each religion insists that it is the only reliable way to God.

Christianity is no exception. In session 3 we looked at some of the exclusive claims Jesus made about himself. The purpose of this session is not to discuss and compare each major religion, but to explain the unique beliefs of Christianity.

After discussing these beliefs, you may want to compare them with other major religions.

The only way to determine whether something is true is to look at the evidence. The facts about Christianity are found in the Bible. The following verses for today express the core of the Christian belief and explain what makes Christianity unique among all other religions.

What the Bible Tells Us

Christ died for us while we were still weak. We were living against God, but at the right time, Christ died for us. Very few people will die to save the life of someone else. Although perhaps for a good man someone might possibly die. But Christ died for us while we were still sinners. In this way God shows his great love for us. (Romans 5:6-8, New Century Version)

God's mercy is great, and he loved us very much. We were spiritually dead because of the things we did wrong against God. But God gave us new life with Christ. You have been saved by God's grace. . . . I mean that you are saved by grace, and you got that grace by believing. You did not save yourselves. It was a gift from God. You cannot brag that you are saved by the work you have done. (Ephesians 2:4-5, 8-9, New Century Version)

How the Bible Relates

1. What did Christ do for us? What is unusual about that?

2. According to Romans 5, what is God's attitude toward us?

3. When you think of the word "sinner," what comes to mind?

4. How much can we do to change our spiritual condition? Who has done the work for us?

5. How does Christianity differ from what other religions teach about getting right with God?

The Bottom Line

The central message of Christianity is this: Jesus died so that imperfect people can have a saving relationship with a perfectly holy God. Furthermore, his resurrection proves that he was unique enough to accomplish this deed.

Prayer

God, if Christianity is truly unique, help me to see it and believe the truth. Amen.

A Final Word

Here is a trustworthy saying that deserves acceptance: Christ came into the world to save sinners. *(The apostle Paul in 1 Timothy 1:15)*

6: The Truth About Christianity

Beginnings

What religious beliefs are you familiar with? Share, if possible, a meaningful religious experience you had as a child. How do you deal with somebody whose religious views differ from yours?

What's Happening Today

North America is a pluralistic culture that includes people from many ethnic and religious backgrounds. As a result, most people have been exposed to people who do not share their religious beliefs.

Certainly the emergence of Islamic fundamentalism on the world scene has made us increasingly aware of that rapidly growing Eastern religion. Adherents of Islam appear on the evening news programs. Millions of faithful Muslims bow toward Mecca several times a day.

Eastern mysticism is becoming popular in Western society, fueled in part by Hollywood stars promoting the mystery of reincarnation. In addition, Eastern meditation has become a regular part of some people's daily routine.

Many of the world's religions have much in common. For example, Christianity, Judaism, Islam, and Mormonism all use sacred writings as part of their religious tradition. Religious figures have played a major part in Buddhism, Islam, Judaism, and Christianity. Most major religious groups have similar codes of conduct, including their own version of the Golden Rule.

For this reason, many people think that all religions worship the same God, although the religions may use different names for God. Some people think that the basic beliefs of all religions are essentially the same.

This is an interesting theory, but a close examination of the world's major religions reveals many essential differences. For example, each religion insists that it is the only reliable way to God.

Christianity is no exception. In session 3 we looked at some of the exclusive claims Jesus made about himself. The purpose of this session is not to discuss and compare each major religion, but to explain the unique beliefs of Christianity.

After discussing these beliefs, you may want to compare them with other major religions.

The only way to determine whether something is true is to look at the evidence. The facts about Christianity are found in the Bible. The following verses for today express the core of the Christian belief and explain what makes Christianity unique among all other religions.

What the Bible Tells Us

Christ died for us while we were still weak. We were living against God, but at the right time, Christ died for us. Very few people will die to save the life of someone else. Although perhaps for a good man someone might possibly die. But Christ died for us while we were still sinners. In this way God shows his great love for us. (Romans 5:6-8, New Century Version)

God's mercy is great, and he loved us very much. We were spiritually dead because of the things we did wrong against God. But God gave us new life with Christ. You have been saved by God's grace. . . . I mean that you are saved by grace, and you got that grace by believing. You did not save yourselves. It was a gift from God. You cannot brag that you are saved by the work you have done. (Ephesians 2:4-5, 8-9, New Century Version)

How the Bible Relates

1. What did Christ do for us? What is unusual about that?

2. According to Romans 5, what is God's attitude toward us?

3. When you think of the word "sinner," what comes to mind?

4. How much can we do to change our spiritual condition? Who has done the work for us?

5. How does Christianity differ from what other religions teach about getting right with God?

The Bottom Line

The central message of Christianity is this: Jesus died so that imperfect people can have a saving relationship with a perfectly holy God. Furthermore, his resurrection proves that he was unique enough to accomplish this deed.

Prayer

God, if Christianity is truly unique, help me to see it and believe the truth. Amen.

A Final Word

Here is a trustworthy saying that deserves acceptance: Christ came into the world to save sinners. *(The apostle Paul in 1 Timothy 1:15)*

6: The Truth About Christianity

Beginnings

What religious beliefs are you familiar with? Share, if possible, a meaningful religious experience you had as a child. How do you deal with somebody whose religious views differ from yours?

What's Happening Today

North America is a pluralistic culture that includes people from many ethnic and religious backgrounds. As a result, most people have been exposed to people who do not share their religious beliefs.

Certainly the emergence of Islamic fundamentalism on the world scene has made us increasingly aware of that rapidly growing Eastern religion. Adherents of Islam appear on the evening news programs. Millions of faithful Muslims bow toward Mecca several times a day.

Eastern mysticism is becoming popular in Western society, fueled in part by Hollywood stars promoting the mystery of reincarnation. In addition, Eastern meditation has become a regular part of some people's daily routine.

Many of the world's religions have much in common. For example, Christianity, Judaism, Islam, and Mormonism all use sacred writings as part of their religious tradition. Religious figures have played a major part in Buddhism, Islam, Judaism, and Christianity. Most major religious groups have similar codes of conduct, including their own version of the Golden Rule.

For this reason, many people think that all religions worship the same God, although the religions may use different names for God. Some people think that the basic beliefs of all religions are essentially the same.

This is an interesting theory, but a close examination of the world's major religions reveals many essential differences. For example, each religion insists that it is the only reliable way to God.

Christianity is no exception. In session 3 we looked at some of the exclusive claims Jesus made about himself. The purpose of this session is not to discuss and compare each major religion, but to explain the unique beliefs of Christianity.

After discussing these beliefs, you may want to compare them with other major religions.

The only way to determine whether something is true is to look at the evidence. The facts about Christianity are found in the Bible. The following verses for today express the core of the Christian belief and explain what makes Christianity unique among all other religions.

What the Bible Tells Us

Christ died for us while we were still weak. We were living against God, but at the right time, Christ died for us. Very few people will die to save the life of someone else. Although perhaps for a good man someone might possibly die. But Christ died for us while we were still sinners. In this way God shows his great love for us. (Romans 5:6-8, New Century Version)

God's mercy is great, and he loved us very much. We were spiritually dead because of the things we did wrong against God. But God gave us new life with Christ. You have been saved by God's grace. . . . I mean that you are saved by grace, and you got that grace by believing. You did not save yourselves. It was a gift from God. You cannot brag that you are saved by the work you have done. (Ephesians 2:4-5, 8-9, New Century Version)

How the Bible Relates

1. What did Christ do for us? What is unusual about that?

2. According to Romans 5, what is God's attitude toward us?

3. When you think of the word "sinner," what comes to mind?

4. How much can we do to change our spiritual condition? Who has done the work for us?

5. How does Christianity differ from what other religions teach about getting right with God?

The Bottom Line

The central message of Christianity is this: Jesus died so that imperfect people can have a saving relationship with a perfectly holy God. Furthermore, his resurrection proves that he was unique enough to accomplish this deed.

Prayer

God, if Christianity is truly unique, help me to see it and believe the truth. Amen.

A Final Word

Here is a trustworthy saying that deserves acceptance: Christ came into the world to save sinners. *(The apostle Paul in 1 Timothy 1:15)*

6: The Truth About Christianity

Beginnings

What religious beliefs are you familiar with? Share, if possible, a meaningful religious experience you had as a child. How do you deal with somebody whose religious views differ from yours?

What's Happening Today

North America is a pluralistic culture that includes people from many ethnic and religious backgrounds. As a result, most people have been exposed to people who do not share their religious beliefs.

Certainly the emergence of Islamic fundamentalism on the world scene has made us increasingly aware of that rapidly growing Eastern religion. Adherents of Islam appear on the evening news programs. Millions of faithful Muslims bow toward Mecca several times a day.

Eastern mysticism is becoming popular in Western society, fueled in part by Hollywood stars promoting the mystery of reincarnation. In addition, Eastern meditation has become a regular part of some people's daily routine.

Many of the world's religions have much in common. For example, Christianity, Judaism, Islam, and Mormonism all use sacred writings as part of their religious tradition. Religious figures have played a major part in Buddhism, Islam, Judaism, and Christianity. Most major religious groups have similar codes of conduct, including their own version of the Golden Rule.

For this reason, many people think that all religions worship the same God, although the religions may use different names for God. Some people think that the basic beliefs of all religions are essentially the same.

This is an interesting theory, but a close examination of the world's major religions reveals many essential differences. For example, each religion insists that it is the only reliable way to God.

Christianity is no exception. In session 3 we looked at some of the exclusive claims Jesus made about himself. The purpose of this session is not to discuss and compare each major religion, but to explain the unique beliefs of Christianity.

After discussing these beliefs, you may want to compare them with other major religions.

The only way to determine whether something is true is to look at the evidence. The facts about Christianity are found in the Bible. The following verses for today express the core of the Christian belief and explain what makes Christianity unique among all other religions.

What the Bible Tells Us

Christ died for us while we were still weak. We were living against God, but at the right time, Christ died for us. Very few people will die to save the life of someone else. Although perhaps for a good man someone might possibly die. But Christ died for us while we were still sinners. In this way God shows his great love for us. (Romans 5:6-8, New Century Version)

God's mercy is great, and he loved us very much. We were spiritually dead because of the things we did wrong against God. But God gave us new life with Christ. You have been saved by God's grace. . . . I mean that you are saved by grace, and you got that grace by believing. You did not save yourselves. It was a gift from God. You cannot brag that you are saved by the work you have done. (Ephesians 2:4-5, 8-9, New Century Version)

How the Bible Relates

1. What did Christ do for us? What is unusual about that?

2. According to Romans 5, what is God's attitude toward us?

3. When you think of the word "sinner," what comes to mind?

4. How much can we do to change our spiritual condition? Who has done the work for us?

5. How does Christianity differ from what other religions teach about getting right with God?

The Bottom Line

The central message of Christianity is this: Jesus died so that imperfect people can have a saving relationship with a perfectly holy God. Furthermore, his resurrection proves that he was unique enough to accomplish this deed.

Prayer

God, if Christianity is truly unique, help me to see it and believe the truth. Amen.

A Final Word

Here is a trustworthy saying that deserves acceptance: Christ came into the world to save sinners. *(The apostle Paul in 1 Timothy 1:15)*

6: The Truth About Christianity

Beginnings

What religious beliefs are you familiar with? Share, if possible, a meaningful religious experience you had as a child. How do you deal with somebody whose religious views differ from yours?

What's Happening Today

North America is a pluralistic culture that includes people from many ethnic and religious backgrounds. As a result, most people have been exposed to people who do not share their religious beliefs.

Certainly the emergence of Islamic fundamentalism on the world scene has made us increasingly aware of that rapidly growing Eastern religion. Adherents of Islam appear on the evening news programs. Millions of faithful Muslims bow toward Mecca several times a day.

Eastern mysticism is becoming popular in Western society, fueled in part by Hollywood stars promoting the mystery of reincarnation. In addition, Eastern meditation has become a regular part of some people's daily routine.

Many of the world's religions have much in common. For example, Christianity, Judaism, Islam, and Mormonism all use sacred writings as part of their religious tradition. Religious figures have played a major part in Buddhism, Islam, Judaism, and Christianity. Most major religious groups have similar codes of conduct, including their own version of the Golden Rule.

For this reason, many people think that all religions worship the same God, although the religions may use different names for God. Some people think that the basic beliefs of all religions are essentially the same.

This is an interesting theory, but a close examination of the world's major religions reveals many essential differences. For example, each religion insists that it is the only reliable way to God.

Christianity is no exception. In session 3 we looked at some of the exclusive claims Jesus made about himself. The purpose of this session is not to discuss and compare each major religion, but to explain the unique beliefs of Christianity.

After discussing these beliefs, you may want to compare them with other major religions.

The only way to determine whether something is true is to look at the evidence. The facts about Christianity are found in the Bible. The following verses for today express the core of the Christian belief and explain what makes Christianity unique among all other religions.

What the Bible Tells Us

Christ died for us while we were still weak. We were living against God, but at the right time, Christ died for us. Very few people will die to save the life of someone else. Although perhaps for a good man someone might possibly die. But Christ died for us while we were still sinners. In this way God shows his great love for us. (Romans 5:6-8, New Century Version)

God's mercy is great, and he loved us very much. We were spiritually dead because of the things we did wrong against God. But God gave us new life with Christ. You have been saved by God's grace. . . . I mean that you are saved by grace, and you got that grace by believing. You did not save yourselves. It was a gift from God. You cannot brag that you are saved by the work you have done. (Ephesians 2:4-5, 8-9, New Century Version)

How the Bible Relates

1. What did Christ do for us? What is unusual about that?

2. According to Romans 5, what is God's attitude toward us?

3. When you think of the word "sinner," what comes to mind?

4. How much can we do to change our spiritual condition? Who has done the work for us?

5. How does Christianity differ from what other religions teach about getting right with God?

The Bottom Line

The central message of Christianity is this: Jesus died so that imperfect people can have a saving relationship with a perfectly holy God. Furthermore, his resurrection proves that he was unique enough to accomplish this deed.

Prayer

God, if Christianity is truly unique, help me to see it and believe the truth. Amen.

A Final Word

Here is a trustworthy saying that deserves acceptance: Christ came into the world to save sinners. *(The apostle Paul in 1 Timothy 1:15)*

6: The Truth About Christianity

Beginnings

What religious beliefs are you familiar with? Share, if possible, a meaningful religious experience you had as a child. How do you deal with somebody whose religious views differ from yours?

What's Happening Today

North America is a pluralistic culture that includes people from many ethnic and religious backgrounds. As a result, most people have been exposed to people who do not share their religious beliefs.

Certainly the emergence of Islamic fundamentalism on the world scene has made us increasingly aware of that rapidly growing Eastern religion. Adherents of Islam appear on the evening news programs. Millions of faithful Muslims bow toward Mecca several times a day.

Eastern mysticism is becoming popular in Western society, fueled in part by Hollywood stars promoting the mystery of reincarnation. In addition, Eastern meditation has become a regular part of some people's daily routine.

Many of the world's religions have much in common. For example, Christianity, Judaism, Islam, and Mormonism all use sacred writings as part of their religious tradition. Religious figures have played a major part in Buddhism, Islam, Judaism, and Christianity. Most major religious groups have similar codes of conduct, including their own version of the Golden Rule.

For this reason, many people think that all religions worship the same God, although the religions may use different names for God. Some people think that the basic beliefs of all religions are essentially the same.

This is an interesting theory, but a close examination of the world's major religions reveals many essential differences. For example, each religion insists that it is the only reliable way to God.

Christianity is no exception. In session 3 we looked at some of the exclusive claims Jesus made about himself. The purpose of this session is not to discuss and compare each major religion, but to explain the unique beliefs of Christianity.

After discussing these beliefs, you may want to compare them with other major religions.

The only way to determine whether something is true is to look at the evidence. The facts about Christianity are found in the Bible. The following verses for today express the core of the Christian belief and explain what makes Christianity unique among all other religions.

What the Bible Tells Us

Christ died for us while we were still weak. We were living against God, but at the right time, Christ died for us. Very few people will die to save the life of someone else. Although perhaps for a good man someone might possibly die. But Christ died for us while we were still sinners. In this way God shows his great love for us. (Romans 5:6-8, New Century Version)

God's mercy is great, and he loved us very much. We were spiritually dead because of the things we did wrong against God. But God gave us new life with Christ. You have been saved by God's grace. . . . I mean that you are saved by grace, and you got that grace by believing. You did not save yourselves. It was a gift from God. You cannot brag that you are saved by the work you have done. (Ephesians 2:4-5, 8-9, New Century Version)

How the Bible Relates

1. What did Christ do for us? What is unusual about that?

2. According to Romans 5, what is God's attitude toward us?

3. When you think of the word "sinner," what comes to mind?

4. How much can we do to change our spiritual condition? Who has done the work for us?

5. How does Christianity differ from what other religions teach about getting right with God?

The Bottom Line

The central message of Christianity is this: Jesus died so that imperfect people can have a saving relationship with a perfectly holy God. Furthermore, his resurrection proves that he was unique enough to accomplish this deed.

Prayer

God, if Christianity is truly unique, help me to see it and believe the truth. Amen.

A Final Word

Here is a trustworthy saying that deserves acceptance: Christ came into the world to save sinners. *(The apostle Paul in 1 Timothy 1:15)*

6: The Truth About Christianity

Beginnings

What religious beliefs are you familiar with? Share, if possible, a meaningful religious experience you had as a child. How do you deal with somebody whose religious views differ from yours?

What's Happening Today

North America is a pluralistic culture that includes people from many ethnic and religious backgrounds. As a result, most people have been exposed to people who do not share their religious beliefs.

Certainly the emergence of Islamic fundamentalism on the world scene has made us increasingly aware of that rapidly growing Eastern religion. Adherents of Islam appear on the evening news programs. Millions of faithful Muslims bow toward Mecca several times a day.

Eastern mysticism is becoming popular in Western society, fueled in part by Hollywood stars promoting the mystery of reincarnation. In addition, Eastern meditation has become a regular part of some people's daily routine.

Many of the world's religions have much in common. For example, Christianity, Judaism, Islam, and Mormonism all use sacred writings as part of their religious tradition. Religious figures have played a major part in Buddhism, Islam, Judaism, and Christianity. Most major religious groups have similar codes of conduct, including their own version of the Golden Rule.

For this reason, many people think that all religions worship the same God, although the religions may use different names for God. Some people think that the basic beliefs of all religions are essentially the same.

This is an interesting theory, but a close examination of the world's major religions reveals many essential differences. For example, each religion insists that it is the only reliable way to God.

Christianity is no exception. In session 3 we looked at some of the exclusive claims Jesus made about himself. The purpose of this session is not to discuss and compare each major religion, but to explain the unique beliefs of Christianity.

After discussing these beliefs, you may want to compare them with other major religions.

The only way to determine whether something is true is to look at the evidence. The facts about Christianity are found in the Bible. The following verses for today express the core of the Christian belief and explain what makes Christianity unique among all other religions.

What the Bible Tells Us

Christ died for us while we were still weak. We were living against God, but at the right time, Christ died for us. Very few people will die to save the life of someone else. Although perhaps for a good man someone might possibly die. But Christ died for us while we were still sinners. In this way God shows his great love for us. (Romans 5:6-8, New Century Version)

God's mercy is great, and he loved us very much. We were spiritually dead because of the things we did wrong against God. But God gave us new life with Christ. You have been saved by God's grace. . . . I mean that you are saved by grace, and you got that grace by believing. You did not save yourselves. It was a gift from God. You cannot brag that you are saved by the work you have done. (Ephesians 2:4-5, 8-9, New Century Version)

How the Bible Relates

1. What did Christ do for us? What is unusual about that?

2. According to Romans 5, what is God's attitude toward us?

3. When you think of the word "sinner," what comes to mind?

4. How much can we do to change our spiritual condition? Who has done the work for us?

5. How does Christianity differ from what other religions teach about getting right with God?

The Bottom Line

The central message of Christianity is this: Jesus died so that imperfect people can have a saving relationship with a perfectly holy God. Furthermore, his resurrection proves that he was unique enough to accomplish this deed.

Prayer

God, if Christianity is truly unique, help me to see it and believe the truth. Amen.

A Final Word

Here is a trustworthy saying that deserves acceptance: Christ came into the world to save sinners. *(The apostle Paul in 1 Timothy 1:15)*

The Whole Truth and Nothing But the Truth

Evaluation Survey

Your response to the Inspirit series is important to us. Please take a moment to give us your reactions to *The Whole Truth and Nothing But the Truth*. Thank you.

Please detach, fold, stamp, and send to
Inspirit
CRC Publications
2850 Kalamazoo Ave. SE
Grand Rapids, MI 49560

	Agree			Disagree	
1. I liked the format of the Inspirit materials.	1	2	3	4	5
2. The theme of the study was relevant for the group.	1	2	3	4	5
3. The Bible passages were appropriate to the themes.	1	2	3	4	5
4. The Bottom Line captured well the central truth of each session.	1	2	3	4	5
5. The theme developed to show the need for Jesus Christ in a person's life.	1	2	3	4	5
6. The leader guide was thorough and helpful.	1	2	3	4	5
7. The truth of the Bible passage remained central in the discussion.	1	2	3	4	5
8. The lessons were the right length.	1	2	3	4	5

9. The thing I liked best about the Inspirit material was . . .

10. If I could change one thing about this study, I would . . .

11. The overall experience of the group was . . .

12. Other topics I'd like to see in this series are . . .

13. Additional comments:

Fold along dotted line and tape together

Place
stamp
here

Inspirit
CRC Publications
2850 Kalamazoo Ave. SE
Grand Rapids, MI 49560